BUILD A TRUSTED BRAND

THE 9-STEP SYSTEM TO
TRANSFORM MARKETING CHAOS,
ATTRACT IDEAL CLIENTS,
AND DRIVE PREDICTABLE GROWTH

Tom Wardman

To my fishy Grandad, Ken Wardman.

For your wisdom, belief, and the lessons that continue to guide me long after you've gone. Your confidence in me never faltered, even when mine did.

This is for you, Grandad—for your influence that continues to shape who I am today.

Contents

Definition

Blueprint

[bloō͵print] *noun*

Something that acts as a plan, model, or template[1].

Foreword

When I first met Tom Wardman, I saw something different.

He wasn't just another marketing professional following the playbook laid out by others. He was someone who truly understood the core principles that elevate marketing from mere tactics to a force that builds trust and drives real, sustained growth.

Over the years, I've seen countless professionals struggle to grasp this concept—focusing on quick wins while neglecting the essential foundation: trust. But Tom got it. He didn't just talk about it; he embodied it.

At IMPACT, we've spent years championing the Endless Customers System™ (formerly *They Ask, You Answer*), guiding businesses to build authority by becoming transparent, honest, and customer centric. It's a journey not for the faint of heart; it requires patience, dedication, and a deep understanding of what it means to earn trust.

So, when I learned that Tom, one of our Certified Partners, was writing *Build a Trusted Brand*, I knew it would be a book that mattered.

Tom is more than just a Certified Partner of IMPACT.

He's someone who has put in the time, learned the strategies, and implemented them with unwavering commitment. His work has consistently proven that he not only grasps these concepts but excels at putting them into practice—for himself and for his clients. He knows the stakes when businesses approach trust as a core pillar of their brand and marketing strategy.

This book isn't just a guide—it's a comprehensive framework drawn from years of experience, research, and success stories that prove trust is not just a buzzword, but the driving force behind sustainable business growth.

Tom shares these insights with clarity, passion, and an authenticity that reflects his hands-on approach. He breaks down the complex landscape of marketing into actionable steps that can transform a company's entire philosophy, not just its campaigns.

Reading *Build a Trusted Brand*, you'll discover why Tom's voice in this space is one you should listen to. He'll take you through the pitfalls most marketers stumble into—from scattershot strategies to short-term thinking—and show you how to replace them with practices that build a strong, resilient brand. His Trust BLUEPRINT™ is simple yet powerful, providing you with tools to not only attract attention but also build lasting, meaningful connections.

If you're ready to make trust the cornerstone of your marketing—and see the profound impact that can have on your business—then you're in the right place.

Tom's insights are as timely as they are timeless, a perfect fit for any business looking to stand out in an ever-crowded marketplace.

It's time to take that journey.

Trust me—it'll be worth it.

- **Bob Ruffolo, CEO, IMPACT.**

PREFACE
The True Currency of Business

Imagine two businesses side by side. Both offer similar products and have comparable prices. Yet one thrives while the other struggles.

One has customers who arrive with purpose, stay longer, and leave satisfied. They return often and speak enthusiastically about their experiences. When problems arise, they give the business the benefit of the doubt. When competitors offer discounts, they remain loyal.

The other business feels different from the moment you approach. Customers enter hesitantly and transactions feel hurried and impersonal. When issues occur, customers become immediately frustrated and demand refunds. Price becomes the primary, and often only factor in their decision-making.

Both businesses work hard.

Both invest in marketing.

Both genuinely want to succeed.

Yet their outcomes couldn't be more different, but **what separates them is a single, powerful factor: trust**.

Trust isn't just a feel-good concept or a fuzzy feeling. It's undeniably the invisible currency that drives every buyer purchasing decision and therefore every successful business transaction.

Whether you're a solopreneur or part of a global enterprise, whether you sell directly to consumers or to other businesses, trust is the foundation upon which the success of your business is built.

The Absence of Trust

Here's a truth that might surprise you: Most businesses are doing trust all wrong. They focus their marketing efforts on themselves, bombarding potential customers with messages like:

- "Buy our latest product!"

- "We're the best in the industry!"

- "Our client came to us with a problem, and we solved it brilliantly!"

Sound familiar? I'll let you in on a secret: I used to be guilty of this approach too.

Picture this: It's 2014, and I'm a fresh-faced university student studying Jazz and Popular Music. I'm launching different bands, cobbling together websites for them, posting occasionally on social media about the gigs we were performing. At the time, I'm thinking I've got marketing all figured out.

Fast forward to my first "real" marketing job, and I'm applying these same misguided principles to a small local accountancy firm, and failing, much to my surprise.

Like many others I came to the realisation that this approach doesn't work. It's like trying to make friends by constantly talking about how great you are.

At best, people tune you out.

At worst, **they actively avoid you.**

The Trust-Building Framework

But what exactly is trust, and why does it wield such transformative power in business?

Trust, at its core, is the confident belief that someone or something will act in your best interests, even when you're not watching.

In personal relationships, we trust friends to keep our secrets, partners to remain faithful, and family members to support us through difficult times.

This trust develops through consistent actions over time, small gestures that demonstrate reliability, honesty, and genuine care for our wellbeing.

Brand trust operates on the same fundamental principles but faces unique challenges.

When you trust a brand, you believe they'll deliver on their promises, treat you fairly, and prioritise your success over their short-term profits. You're confident that their products will work as advertised, their customer service will resolve issues promptly, and their values align with your own.

Consider how you feel about brands you truly trust. Perhaps it's the local mechanic who explains exactly what's wrong with your car, shows you the faulty part, and only recommends necessary repairs.

Or the software company that proactively notifies you about security issues and provides clear, jargon-free solutions. These businesses don't just sell products, but they also earn your confidence through transparency, expertise, and genuine concern for your experience.

Trusted brands ultimately enjoy remarkable advantages: customers pay premium prices willingly, forgive occasional mistakes gracefully, and become passionate advocates who drive new business through word-of-mouth recommendations.

They've transcended the commodity trap where price becomes the only differentiator.

As I looked deeper into the world of content and inbound marketing, I stumbled upon something profound: Regardless of tactics or trends, the underlying goal of your marketing efforts is always the same—to build a trusted brand.

But how do you *actually* do that?

How can you create a marketing strategy that genuinely builds trust, without relying on outside help or getting lost in a sea of conflicting advice?

That's why I wrote this book.

Within these pages, you'll find a **framework of nine steps that, when followed in order, will help you create a sales and marketing plan focused on what really matters**: Your target audience, their pain points, and the questions they're asking and helping them make the most informed and well-education buying decision possible.

Each step will guide you through:

1. The underlying theory

2. Practical implementation strategies

3. Answers to common questions

4. Insights from field experts (in select chapters)

The Marketing Plan Myth

Creating an effective marketing plan is far more challenging than most people realise.

Many business owners and marketers (much like I was in my early days) believe a marketing plan is just a handful of blog post ideas and some sporadic social media posts.

This misconception leads to a dangerous cycle:

1. Business owners hire marketing managers without understanding what they need.

2. They provide inadequate support and resources.

3. They become frustrated by the lack of results—results that were nearly impossible to achieve given the circumstances.

Your Path to Marketing Success

The final chapters of this book provide key success factors and additional resources to help you act on what you've learned.

Remember, the goal isn't just to understand the principles of trust-building marketing—it's to apply them and see real results in your business.

Building a trusted brand isn't a quick fix or a magic bullet. It requires consistent effort and a willingness to play the long game. But the payoff can be astronomical: a steady stream of leads, loyal customers, and a reputation that precedes you.

This book aims to give you a system for building trust that will elevate your entire approach to marketing.

Remember, in the world of business, trust isn't just important—it's everything.

Who This Book Isn't For

Before we begin this journey together, it's important to be clear about who this book is designed to help—and equally important, who it isn't for.

Effective marketing is about acting and making a long-term commitment to serving your audience with helpful content. Without this commitment, you're setting yourself up for failure before you've even begun.

Moreover, if you approach marketing with a "it won't work" mindset, you're right—it won't. A defeatist attitude will rob you of the willpower and determination needed to successfully implement the frameworks in this book.

Ask yourself the following questions:

- Should we be honest and open with our potential customers?

- Should we transparently answer our customers' questions?

- Should our potential customers feel well-informed and satisfied when they visit our website?

- Should we produce content that our sales team can integrate into every sales process and funnel we have?

If you answered "no" to any of these, it might be time to reconsider your approach to marketing and sales.

But if you answered "yes" to these questions, congratulations! This book is here to help you make that vision a reality.

We're about to embark on a journey to transform your marketing from a series of disjointed tactics into a cohesive strategy that builds trust, nurtures relationships, and ultimately drives growth.

Let's begin.

A Note from the Author

Thank you for picking up this book. If these ideas have sparked something in you, or if you're wondering how to put these strategies into action, please get in touch. I'd love to hear your story.

You can contact me directly at: tom@tomwardman.com.

I'll aim to reply personally and promptly. I'm genuinely excited to hear about the trust you build and the success you create!

PART 1
Building Strong Foundations for Marketing Success

CHAPTER 1

The Trust Deficit: Identifying Gaps in Traditional Marketing Approaches

Let's face it: marketing is hard. Really hard.

If you're reading this book, chances are you've hit a wall with your marketing efforts. Maybe you've tried everything from social media blitzes to email campaigns, yet any results remain elusive, frustrating you, your team, and the leadership around you.

You're not alone. In fact, you're in good company.

As someone who's been in the trenches of marketing for years, I've seen firsthand the immense pressure marketing teams face. Business leaders demand fresh ideas, tangible results, and a clear return on investment. They often do so without truly understanding the complexity of the task at hand.

That's a tall order, and one that often boils down to a single, deceptively simple directive: generate leads.

"We want more leads!" everyone cried. Easier said than done, am I right?

Here's the kicker: **generating leads in what has become an increasingly saturated market isn't just about shouting louder than your competitors or throwing money at the latest marketing fad**.

It's about building trust. And trust, as it turns out, is in short supply.

The Four Pillars of Marketing Frustration

Through my work, I've identified four primary challenges that repeatedly crop up. These are the trust-eroding pillars that can turn even the most well-intentioned marketing plan into a fruitless exercise:

1. **The scattergun approach**: Trying every tactic under the sun without a cohesive strategy.

2. **The short-term sight**: Thinking without any form of long-term strategy and quickly pivoting without any chance for real results or return.

3. **The old-school thinking**: Relying solely on, and sometimes rigidly adhering to, traditional marketing efforts such as cold calling.

4. **The planning vacuum**: Failing to create any form of marketing plan.

As we delve deeper into each of these challenges in the coming chapters, I encourage you to reflect on which resonate most strongly with your experience.

Why? Because identifying your primary stumbling block is the first step towards overcoming it.

This is not me calling out where you might have gone wrong. Rather, it is about helping you reflect on your own experiences so you can apply the learnings from this book and succeed in the future.

Now let's turn the page and face reality, shall we?

The Compound Effect of Consistency

Now, let's flip the script.

Imagine your marketing efforts as a snowball rolling down a hill. Each consistent action—whether a blog post, a social media update, or an email newsletter—adds a layer to that snowball. Over time, it grows, picks up speed, and becomes an unstoppable force.

This is the power of consistent marketing. It is not about grand, one-off gestures. It is about small, regular actions that build momentum over time:

- Your website becomes a regularly updated hub of valuable information.

- Your content marketing establishes you as a thought leader in your industry.

- Your social media presence becomes a reliable source of insights for your audience.

- Your email list grows steadily, filled with engaged subscribers who genuinely want to hear from you.

Remember, **trust is not built overnight.** It is cultivated through consistent, valuable interactions over time.

From Haphazard to Habitual: Making the Shift

So, how do you break free from the cycle of haphazard marketing? Here are a few steps to get you started:

- **Commit to a realistic schedule**: It is better to post one high-quality blog post a month consistently than to aim for weekly posts and burn out after a month.

- **Create a content calendar**: Plan your marketing activities in advance. This bird's-eye view helps maintain consistency and aligns your efforts with business goals.

- **Batch create content**: Set aside dedicated time to create multiple pieces of content at once. This ensures you always have a backlog of material ready to go.

- **Automate where possible**: Use scheduling tools for social media posts and email newsletters. Consistency does not mean you need to post manually every day.

- **Measure and adjust**: Regularly review your efforts. What is working? What is not? Use these insights to refine your strategy rather than abandon it entirely.

Your audience craves reliability. They want to visit your website or social media profiles and think, "This company knows what they're doing. I'm in safe hands."

So do not be the business that cuts its marketing lifeline at the first sign of trouble. Instead, commit to consistency. Give your marketing team the time, resources, and trust they need to implement a steady, long-term strategy.

Your future self will thank you for it.

Chapter Summary

- Marketing efforts must be steady and reliable to build trust. Sporadic activities harm brand credibility and waste resources.

- Inconsistent marketing creates multiple problems: reduced authority, customer confusion, inefficient spending, and difficulties measuring success.

- Consistent marketing builds momentum over time through regular, valuable interactions with your audience.

- Success requires moving from random activities to habitual practices through realistic scheduling, content planning, and strategic automation.

- Long-term marketing success comes from maintaining a steady approach rather than occasional bursts of intense activity.

CHAPTER 3

The Long Game: Why Short-Term Marketing is a Losing Strategy

There's a certain irony that exists in the world of marketing: many businesses' long-term strategies are a series of short-term failures strung together. They hop from one tactic to the next, such as content marketing one month and social media the next, never giving any approach enough time to bear fruit.

This doom loop destroys trust, and it is sadly an approach that is alarmingly common. At its core, this short-term mindset reveals a fundamental misunderstanding of how trust works.

Let's use a dating analogy. Imagine walking into a bar and proposing marriage to every person you meet.

It sounds ridiculous, doesn't it? Yet this is essentially what businesses do when they expect immediate results from their marketing efforts.

The Hidden Message in Short-Term Thinking

Marketing, like any meaningful relationship, is built on trust. **And that takes time.**

Think about your buyers. They are savvier than ever, armed with search engines and an insatiable appetite for information. They are not looking for a quick fling with your brand. They are searching for a long-term relationship built on trust, value, and mutual understanding.

When you engage in short-term marketing tactics, you are sending a message—and it is not the one you want to promote.

Put yourself in your potential customer's shoes for a moment. They come across your sporadic blog posts or your abandoned social media accounts. What conclusions might they draw? If you cannot commit to your own marketing efforts, how can they trust you to commit to solving their problems?

It is a harsh truth, but one worth facing. **Your half-hearted marketing efforts could be driving potential customers straight into the arms of your more consistent competitors**.

The "We've Tried Marketing" Myth

Similarly, here is a phrase I hear all too often: "We've tried marketing. It doesn't work for us."

Let's be clear. If you have only given your marketing efforts a few months to yield results, you have not really tried marketing at all. You have merely dipped your toe in the water and decided the entire ocean is too cold.

Good marketing needs time to mature. The businesses I have seen achieve remarkable results are not the ones looking for quick wins. They are the ones that have committed to consistent marketing efforts for 12, 18, or even 24 months or more.

These businesses understand that marketing is not just about immediate lead generation. It is about:

- Building brand awareness
- Establishing thought leadership
- Creating valuable resources for potential customers
- Nurturing relationships over time

In other words, it is about playing the long game.

Embracing the Long Game: A Roadmap

So, how do you shift from short-term thinking to a long-term, trust-building marketing strategy?

The foundation of any successful long-term marketing approach is this: **focus on value above all else.**

Every piece of content, every social media post, and every email should provide genuine value to your audience. When value becomes your guiding principle, all other decisions become clearer.

Trust is not built through frequency or persistence alone. It is built through consistently delivering something worthwhile. This principle should guide every marketing decision you make.

- **Set realistic expectations**: Understand that meaningful results take time. Do not expect miracles in the first few months.

- **Commit to consistency**: Develop a content calendar and stick to it. Consistency builds trust.

- **Diversify your efforts**: Do not put all your eggs in one basket. Use a variety of marketing channels that suit your audience.

- **Monitor and adjust**: Review your efforts regularly but avoid making reactive decisions based on short-term fluctuations.

- **Educate stakeholders**: Ensure everyone in your organisation understands the long-term nature of effective marketing.

- **Celebrate small wins**: While keeping your eye on the long-term goal, acknowledge and celebrate incremental progress.

The Payoff: Why the Long Game Wins

Businesses that embrace long-term marketing strategies gain rewards that extend far beyond lead generation:

- **Brand authority**: Over time, you become the trusted resource in your industry.

- **Customer loyalty**: Trust-based relationships lead to repeat business and referrals.

- **Reduced marketing costs**: As your organic reach grows, the cost per lead typically decreases.

- **Competitive advantage**: While others chase trends, you create a sustainable and reliable marketing foundation.

Patience Pays

The businesses that succeed are not those searching for overnight success, but those committed to playing the long game.

If you are ready to nurture your efforts with consistency and patience, you are on the path to creating a marketing strategy that does more than generate leads. You are building a brand that can stand the test of time.

Remember, in marketing—as in life—good things come to those who wait and work consistently towards their goals.

_____ *Chapter Summary* _____

- Short-term marketing creates a cycle of failure. Jumping between tactics without allowing time for results undermines progress.

- Building customer trust requires patience and consistency. Like any relationship, it cannot be rushed.

- Successful marketing needs time to grow. The best results come from businesses that commit to efforts over 12 to 24 months.

- A long-term strategy needs realistic goals, consistent action, and careful review without reactive decisions.

- Patient, ongoing marketing builds real rewards: strong brand authority, loyal customers, and long-term cost efficiency.

CHAPTER 4

From Cold Calls to Warm Connections: The Power of Authentic Marketing

"But Tom," you might be thinking, "our transactional marketing is working just fine!"

Well, before you close this book, let me ask you this: **are you building relationships, or just chasing transactions?**

In this chapter, we're going to examine transactional marketing through a crucial lens—one that will redefine your approach to customer relationships. That lens is trust.

As we'll explore throughout this book, building trust through your marketing is about educating your audience, solving their problems, and empowering them to make informed decisions. But, as we established in the last chapter, trust takes time to build.

Transactional marketing often tries to shortcut this process. It's like trying to microwave a gourmet meal—you might get something that looks like food, but it lacks depth and flavour.

The Downsides of the 'Instant Trust' Approach

When you rely solely on methods like cold calling or mass mailings, you're asking leads to go from "Who are you?" to "Take my money!" in the blink of an eye. It's a leap most people aren't willing to make.

Let's break down why this approach often falls flat:

- **Lack of context**: Your audience has no frame of reference for who you are or why they should care.

- **Interruption, not invitation**: You're forcing your way into their day, not being invited in.

- **One-size-fits-all messaging**: You're not addressing their specific needs or pain points.

- **Focus on selling, not helping**: Your message is all about you, not about how you can solve their problems.

It's also increasingly self-centred. You're shouting "me, me, me"—showcasing your products, trumpeting your achievements, but rarely addressing your audience's needs and pain points.

Without consistent, valuable content and a well-maintained online presence, you're operating in a trust vacuum. **There's no authoritative voice building a relationship, no helpful resources guiding potential customers through their decision-making process.**

In this vacuum, your sporadic transactional marketing efforts are like shouting into the void. You might occasionally get an echo back, but you're not building anything sustainable. Worse still, you open your business up to the failings of the inconsistent habits we talked about a couple of chapters ago.

Bridging the Gap: From Traditional to Trust-Based Marketing

Now, I'm not suggesting you need to abandon transactional marketing entirely. Instead, think of it as one tool in your wider marketing arsenal.

If you pair that with the tactics and frameworks outlined in this book, you're building consistency and showing a genuine commitment to your audience's needs. And believe me, the payoff is immense, bringing you:

- **Loyal customers**: People who trust you are more likely to stick with you long term.

- **Word-of-mouth marketing**: Trusted brands get talked about and recommended.

- **Higher conversion rates**: When people trust you, they're more likely to buy from you.

- **Premium pricing**: Trust allows you to command higher prices for your products or services.

- **Resilience**: Trusted brands can weather market changes and challenges more easily.

In the end, the most successful businesses aren't those that make the most sales calls or send the most flyers. They're the ones that build the most trust.

By shifting from a transactional, short-term approach to an authentic, trust-building strategy, you're not just changing your marketing tactics. You're transforming your entire business philosophy.

So, are you ready to stop interrupting and start connecting?

The path to becoming a trusted brand starts with a single step—and that step is choosing to prioritise your audience's needs over your desire for a quick sale.

_____ *Chapter Summary* _____

- Transactional marketing often seeks instant trust, asking customers to move from stranger to buyer too quickly without building real connections.

- Successful modern marketing requires moving beyond self-centred messages to focus on solving customer problems and providing genuine value.

- Trust-building marketing combines multiple approaches, including helpful content, genuine social engagement, targeted email nurturing, and more.

- Building trust takes time but delivers significant rewards: loyal customers, organic referrals, improved conversion rates, and greater pricing power.

- The shift from transaction-focused to trust-focused marketing requires patience, consistency, and a genuine commitment to serving customer needs.

CHAPTER 5

The 'Star Wars' Marketing Strategy: Why Planning is Your Secret Weapon

In the vast galaxy of marketing analogies, we've heard it all before: the "ostrich strategy" of burying your head in the sand when problems arise, or the "butterfly effect" of small changes leading to big results.

But today, we're going to explore a marketing strategy that's out of this world—quite literally.

Welcome to the *Star Wars* Marketing Strategy.

Star Wars isn't just one of the biggest media franchises in history; it's a masterclass in the power of planning—or sometimes, the lack thereof. Whether you're a die-hard fan or you've somehow managed to avoid the cultural phenomenon entirely, there's a crucial marketing lesson hidden within those iconic yellow scrolling texts.

The Plot Twist That Wasn't Planned

Let's start with arguably the most famous plot twist in cinema history: "No, I am your father."

My inner child still experiences a jaw drop every time I think of the line spoken by Darth Vader. It's a line that sent shockwaves through audiences worldwide. But here's the kicker—**it was never part of the original plan**.

George Lucas, the mastermind behind *Star Wars*, initially intended to make just one film. The original *Star Wars* (later retroactively titled *Episode IV: A New Hope*) was meant to be a standalone story. It was only after its monumental success that Lucas retroactively labelled it *Episode IV* and continued the saga.

This lack of long-term planning led to some narrative gymnastics in the following films. In *Episode IV*, Obi-Wan told Luke that Darth Vader had murdered Luke's father. But then, two films later, we witness Obi-Wan's awkward explanation in *Episode VI: Return of the Jedi* about Vader killing Luke's father being true "from a certain point of view."

That's the **storytelling equivalent of a marketing team scrambling to explain inconsistent messaging**.

The Sequel Trilogy: When Too Many Cooks Spoil the Broth

Fast forward to the recent Sequel Trilogy, and we see another, arguably worse, planning pitfall. Disney's approach was to give each director creative freedom, resulting in narrative whiplash between films.

Rian Johnson's *Episode VIII: The Last Jedi* took the story in bold new directions, subverting fan expectations. The fan reception to this was extremely divisive. However, the original director for *Episode IX* had every intention of continuing the narrative, as Johnson had done with J.J. Abrams' *Episode VII: The Force Awakens*.

But when J.J. Abrams returned for what became *Episode IX: The Rise of Skywalker*, taking over the directorship from Colin Trevorrow, he attempted to course-correct and appease disappointed fans.

The result? A final film that felt more like a hasty retcon than a satisfying conclusion.

This is **akin to a marketing team changing its core message with every campaign**, leaving the audience confused and disconnected.

The Prequel Trilogy: Why Planning Prevails

Now, here's an unpopular opinion that illustrates the point perfectly: the Prequel Trilogy—*Episodes I–III*—is the most coherent from a storytelling perspective. Why? Because Lucas had a plan from the outset.

Despite their flaws—of which there are many—these films tell a consistent story across three movies. Lucas knew the beginning, middle, and end before he ever yelled "Action!" on the set of *Episode I: The Phantom Menace*.

So, what does all this space opera drama have to do with your marketing strategy? Everything.

1. **Have a long-term vision**: Don't just focus on your next campaign. Think about where you want your brand to be in three, five, or even ten years—and write it down. Resist defining this vision in sales figures alone. Instead, imagine what people would say about your brand. How would customers describe you? What reputation would you have? This narrative vision becomes your North Star for every marketing decision.

2. **Maintain consistency**: Ensure your messaging remains consistent across all platforms and over time. Don't pull a "certain point of view" on your audience.

3. **Plan for contingencies**: The market can change rapidly. Have plans in place for different scenarios so you're not caught off guard.

4. **Collaborate, but with direction**: Input from different team members is valuable but ensure there's a unified vision guiding all efforts.

5. **Be prepared to adapt**: While planning is crucial, be ready to adjust your strategy based on audience feedback and market changes. Just ensure these adjustments align with your overall goals.

6. **Don't retcon your brand**: If you need to evolve your brand, do it thoughtfully and transparently. Don't try to pretend previous messaging never happened.

The Force of Planning Compels You

In marketing, failing to plan is planning to fail. Without a coherent strategy, your marketing efforts risk becoming a disjointed series of campaigns, each potentially contradicting the last.

Remember, your audience is along for the journey. They're investing their time, attention, and potentially their money in your brand story.

Instead, have a clear vision, a well-thought-out plan, and the flexibility to adapt. With this approach, you won't just survive in the competitive galaxy of modern business—you'll thrive.

May the force of strategic planning be with you. Always.

_____ *Chapter Summary* _____

- Like *Star Wars'* narrative challenges, a lack of long-term planning in marketing can result in confused messaging and audience disconnect.

- Changing direction too frequently creates a disjointed experience. Consistency is essential for maintaining audience trust.

- Having a clear long-term vision ensures coherent messaging across all marketing activities and campaigns.

- While planning is vital, flexibility to adapt within the framework of overarching goals is equally important.

- Successful marketing requires balancing collaborative input with a unified direction to deliver a consistent brand story.

CHAPTER 6

Who This Book Is For: Mastering the Zero Moment of Truth

You've picked up this book because you're facing marketing challenges. But before we look at solutions, let's talk about mindset.

For this book to be more than just words on a page—for it to become a blueprint for real change—you need to embrace a specific outlook. That outlook is: "I want to master my Zero Moment of Truth."

"Zero Moment of Truth?" I hear you ask.

It's a phrase coined by Google, defining the extensive research phase buyers undertake before they ever contact a company. And when I say *extensive*, I mean it.

The Zero Moment of Truth represents that crucial window when potential customers actively research solutions to their problems.

They're reading reviews, comparing options, watching videos, downloading guides, and forming opinions about different companies—all before making any direct contact.

This isn't casual browsing; it's **serious evaluation**.

They're building a shortlist, eliminating options, and often arriving at a preferred choice before they ever pick up the phone or fill out a contact form.

On average, 80% of the buying decision is made online before a prospect even thinks about reaching out. And that percentage is continuing to grow.

The Evolution of Buying Behaviour

The way people buy is changing faster than ever before. Let's rewind to the early days of the internet. Back then, how much of the buying process was completed before a prospect reached out?

It was likely around 20%—maybe less.

But here's the kicker: that number isn't going to retreat.

If anything, it's set to rise.

In some industries, it might already be higher—remember, 80% is just the average. Take food delivery apps like UberEats and Just Eat, for instance. They've pushed that number to 100%—the entire buying decision is made online before you even contact your favourite restaurant.

So, why are businesses making more of their buying decisions before that first contact? The answer boils down to one fundamental principle that unites every business on the planet: trust.

Regardless of how you classify your business—B2B, B2C, charitable, non-profit, or anything else—**trust is going to be fundamental to your success. We're all in the business of building trust. It's an eternal principle with no beginning, middle, or end**.

The problem? We don't talk about trust nearly enough. Yet, if you build a business around this principle, you're setting yourself up for long-term success.

A Fundamental Shift in the Buyer's Journey

The internet hasn't just changed how we shop—it has fundamentally altered the entire buyer's journey.

Flashback to the early days of the internet. The buying journey was very different. You would see an advert, visit a shop, speak to a sales rep, make your purchase, and subsequently enjoy it. Your First Moment of Truth would be that in-store experience, and the percentage of the buying decision made online was likely around 10–15%, or even lower.

Fast forward to today. After seeing an advert, your next step is to research extensively online—the Zero Moment of Truth—and only then might you visit a shop and make that purchase.

This new step—the online research phase—has become the linchpin of the modern buying process. Consumers are judging companies online before making decisions offline. In fact, **research shows that buyers typically consume ten pieces of content before purchasing from a company.**

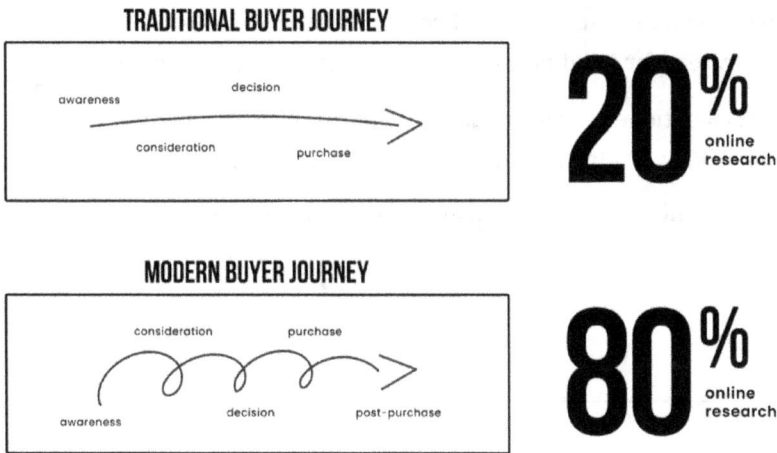

TRADITIONAL BUYER JOURNEY

awareness

decision

consideration

purchase

20% online research

MODERN BUYER JOURNEY

consideration

purchase

awareness

decision

post-purchase

80% online research

The Blurring Lines of Sales and Marketing

This seismic shift in buyer behaviour has profound implications for how businesses operate. **Gone are the days when sales and marketing could function in isolation**, with marketing purely focused on brand growth and sales driving revenue.

Today, marketing plays a crucial role in the actual sale. It's now marketing's job to answer questions, build trust, and influence the buying decision. Sales doesn't replace this; rather, it accentuates it, with marketing content working in tandem with your sales team and processes.

The divide between sales and marketing is disappearing, and this trend is only set to continue. In the coming years, we might see 90% or even 100% of the buying decision made before a consumer reaches out.

Put simply, if you're not consistently publishing content online, in the eyes of your consumers, you might as well not exist!

So, when we talk about the mindset needed for your marketing efforts to truly work, we're talking about embracing the determination to master your Zero Moment of Truth. It's about being prepared to use marketing as a long-term strategy for building trust and relationships with your audience.

As I mentioned in the preface, this approach won't work if you're looking for quick fixes or planning to take a passive approach to your marketing.

But if this resonates with you, you're in the right place.

Keep reading!

Chapter Summary

- Today's buyers make up to 80% of their purchasing decisions online before contacting companies—and this percentage is only increasing, with some industries already reaching 100%.

- The traditional buying journey has fundamentally shifted, with the Zero Moment of Truth (extensive online research) now taking place before any direct contact.

- Trust is the fundamental principle driving this evolution in buying behaviour, uniting businesses of all types, regardless of sector.

- Sales and marketing roles are merging, as marketing content plays an increasingly crucial role in building trust and influencing purchasing decisions.

- Success requires embracing this new reality and committing to honest, transparent content that genuinely informs potential customers.

PART 2

The 9-Step System To Building Trust With Your Audience

CHAPTER 7

The Trust BLUEPRINT™: Your Guide Through Marketing Overwhelm

The **Trust BLUEPRINT™** was born out of a single frustration: overwhelm.

It's a problem I keep encountering with businesses from all walks of life. You're not just struggling to implement a marketing plan—you're grappling with creating one in the first place. The marketing world has become so vast and complex that knowing where to start is anybody's guess.

This paralysis by analysis has led to inaction. When you're drowning in options, you choose to do nothing rather than risk doing the wrong thing. The result? Missed opportunities and stagnant growth.

That's why this book exists. It is designed to be your guiding light through the fog of marketing possibilities—a step-by-step framework that makes sense of the madness.

But let's be clear: **this isn't a magic wand or a quick fix.**

The Trust BLUEPRINT™ is a strategy—a roadmap that requires dedication and effort to implement. It's not about cutting corners; it's about building a solid foundation for long-term success.

Let me also be clear when I say that implementing this framework isn't a solitary journey. Once you've finished this book, I recommend gathering your team together—specifically anyone involved in marketing, sales, or customer relations. Whether you have a full-fledged marketing department or a single in-house marketer, collective buy-in is crucial.

Set aside time to strategise together. Discuss how the Trust BLUEPRINT™ can be tailored to your specific business needs. Remember, this is a collaborative process. The more minds you have working on it, the richer and more effective your marketing plan will be.

If you and your team commit to this process, I can promise you that, when implemented correctly, the Trust BLUEPRINT™ can transform your marketing efforts. You'll create a steady stream of well-qualified leads who already trust your brand and are primed to become customers.

Isn't that what we're all after in business?

The 9 Steps of the Trust BLUEPRINT™

Without further ado, let's unveil the structure of the Trust BLUEPRINT™. It consists of nine key steps:

1. **Buyer**: Creating detailed personas that go beyond demographics to understand your ideal customers' real motivations and challenges.

2. **Learning**: Becoming your industry's most helpful teacher by obsessing over the questions your customers are actually asking.

3. **Understanding**: Building transparency through operational openness and honest pricing discussions that competitors avoid.

4. **Engagement**: Creating meaningful connections through lead capture, social media, and zero-click content that provides instant value.

5. **Pipeline**: Designing customer journeys that guide prospects naturally from awareness to advocacy without feeling pushy.

6. **Repurpose**: Transforming one piece of content into multiple formats to maximise reach while maintaining your core message.

7. **Impact**: Using story-driven marketing that positions your customers as heroes rather than promoting yourself.

8. **Negatives**: Embracing the power of honest communication about limitations and who you're not right for.

9. **Time**: Building sustainable systems that compound over months and years rather than chasing quick wins.

Each of these steps is a crucial piece of the puzzle, designed to work in harmony to create a comprehensive, effective marketing strategy.

In the following chapters, we'll dive deep into each of these steps. We'll explore what they mean, why they're important, and how you can implement them in your business.

Are you ready to cut through the marketing noise and build a strategy that truly resonates with your audience? Are you prepared to put in the work to create a marketing plan that doesn't just attract leads, but builds lasting trust?

If so, turn the page. **Your journey to mastering the Trust BLUEPRINT™ starts now.**

Chapter Summary

- Many businesses struggle with marketing paralysis, overwhelmed by options and afraid of making the wrong choices.

- The Trust BLUEPRINT™ provides a structured framework to guide marketing decisions and implementation.

- Success requires team collaboration and buy-in from everyone involved in marketing, sales, and customer relations.

- The framework consists of nine key steps: Buyer, Learning, Understanding, Engagement, Pipeline, Repurpose, Impact, Negatives, and Time.

- When properly implemented, this structured approach helps build trust and generate qualified leads who are ready to become customers.

THE TRUST BLUEPRINT ™

1 Buyer
Define Your Ideal Customer

Create detailed buyer personas to understand your ideal customer's real problems, motivations, and decision-making process.

2 Learning
Educate Your Market

Become your industry's best teacher by obsessing over your customers' questions and creating content to answer them.

3 Understanding
Reveal Your Process

Pull back the curtain on your operations, pricing, and processes to help prospects understand what working with you actually looks like.

4 Engagement
Connect Authentically

Build meaningful connections through lead capture, social media, and zero-click content.

5 Pipeline
Guide the Journey

Design a customer journey that guides prospects naturally from awareness through decision with the right content at each stage.

6 Repurpose
Multiply Your Content

Transform your existing content into multiple formats and platforms to maximise reach while maintaining consistent messaging.

7 Impact
Tell Compelling Stories

Use story-driven marketing to turn case studies and testimonials into compelling success stories.

8 Negatives
Embrace Radical Honesty

Build trust through radical honesty by addressing problems, limitations, and who you are NOT a fit for.

9 Time
Build for the Long Term

Create sustainable marketing systems with a long-term mindset, proper team alignment, and consistent measurement.

CHAPTER 8

BLUEPRINT Step 1: Buyer - Know Your Customer, Know Your Success

"We target small business owners aged 35–55..."

Stop right there.

A buyer persona should not sound like a dating profile, because knowing your customer's age and job title is about as useful as knowing their star sign.

In the chapters ahead, we're going to explore the foundation of all successful marketing: truly understanding who you're talking to. Not just their demographics, but their dreams, their fears, their late-night Google searches.

In the upcoming chapters, we'll dive deep into creating buyer personas. You'll learn why most businesses get them completely wrong, how to create personas that drive decisions, and why the best marketing often starts with knowing who you *don't* want to work with.

We'll tackle the common myths about buyer personas, show you how to turn dry data into actionable insights, and demonstrate why understanding your ideal customer is about much more than just marketing it's about transforming your entire business.

Without a clear target, you're just shooting in the dark. That's exactly where most businesses find themselves. They're armed with great products and services but no clear picture of who they're trying to reach.

But when you truly understand who you're trying to reach, every other decision becomes clearer.

If you're ready to turn your vague idea of a target market into a crystal-clear picture of your ideal customer, then turn the page.

CHAPTER 9

Creating Compelling Buyer Personas: The Foundation of Targeted Marketing

Like archery, without a clear target, all your skill and preparation is for nothing. This is precisely the predicament many businesses find themselves in when they approach marketing without well-defined buyer personas.

Now, I recognise that the mere mention of "buyer personas" might make you throw up a little in your mouth; after all, they've gotten a bad rap in recent years. As inbound and content marketing became more widely adopted, it seems everybody felt the need to create buyer personas for their strategy—and for good reason.

But the truth is, buyer personas are a misunderstood concept, and most businesses get them completely wrong.

Businesses know that they need buyer personas, but in their rush to tick that box, they often create caricatures rather than characters. They end up with the marketing equivalent of a cardboard cut-out instead of a living, breathing representation of their ideal customer.

To ensure your marketing plan gets off to the best possible footing, you need to come back to the fundamental question: "Who do we want to target?" It's a simple question, but the answer can transform your entire approach to marketing.

What is a Buyer Persona?

Let's start with a definition. There is a plethora of them out there, but in my opinion, HubSpot has provided the most concise and accurate:

"A buyer persona is a semi-fictional representation of your ideal customer based on market research and real data about your existing customers."

Now, let's break this down further:

1. **Semi-fictional:** This is crucial. Your personas should be grounded in reality, not fantasy.

2. **Ideal customer:** We're not talking about any customer, but your best customers.

3. **Market research:** This isn't guesswork. It requires digging into data and trends.

4. **Real data about existing customers:** The best insights often come from those already buying from you.

Now, you're probably wondering what makes a customer your *best*.

It's not always the most obvious answer.

Your best customers might be those who spend the most money, but they could also be the ones who refer others most frequently, require the least support, stay loyal the longest, or provide the most valuable feedback.

Consider factors like profitability (not just revenue), ease of working with, alignment with your values, growth potential, and their likelihood to become advocates for your business.

If you're launching a new company or product, you won't have this data yet—and that's perfectly normal.

In this case, start with educated assumptions based on market research, competitor analysis, and your business model.

Who do you believe would get the most value from what you offer? What type of customer would be most likely to pay your prices and appreciate your approach?

You can always refine these assumptions as you gather real customer data.

Common Mistakes When Creating Buyer Personas

Before we dive into how to create effective buyer personas, let's talk about where many businesses go wrong—because recognising these pitfalls is the first step to avoiding them.

First, and most frankly, you're not writing a novel. **Many businesses create completely fictionalised accounts of their utopian clients**. They craft elaborate backstories and quirky details that have no basis in reality. It's like writing a character for a novel instead of a tool for business strategy.

Your audience isn't fiction, and neither are their problems. The questions they type into Google are real, their pain points are real, and your solutions need to be real too.

Another common mistake is treating buyer personas like a one-time task and moving on to the next big thing. Businesses spend time creating their personas, pat themselves on the back, and then let those carefully crafted profiles gather dust.

Your audience is constantly evolving. Their needs change, their behaviours shift, and if your personas don't keep up, you'll find yourself marketing to ghosts of customers past.

The next mistake is around using your personas in practice. Even businesses that create solid, data-based personas often fail to use them effectively. They have beautiful buyer persona documents that never leave the marketing folder on their shared drive.

Your personas should be living, breathing parts of your strategy. They should inform every marketing decision, every piece of content, every sales approach. If they're not, you're missing out on their true power.

The Buyer Persona Template: A Step-by-Step Guide

Now that we understand what buyer personas are and where businesses often go wrong, let's roll up our sleeves and get into the nitty-gritty of creating effective personas.

Step 1: Gather Your Team

If you're a solo marketer hoping to create buyer personas on your own, you're already fighting a losing battle. Creating buyer personas isn't a solo sport. It's a team effort that should involve multiple departments.

Here's the crux: your marketing team understands broader market trends and the competitor landscape. The flipside of that coin is the sales team, who have direct interactions with prospects and understand their immediate pain points.

But beyond that, customer service and product development teams can play a key role in the creation of buyer personas too. Customer service knows the questions and challenges that come up post-purchase, and product development teams can provide insights into the problems your product or service solves.

By bringing these perspectives together, you create a more holistic and accurate persona.

Step 2: Mine Your Existing Data

Before you start reaching out to customers or conducting new research, look at the data you already have. This might include:

- Customer purchase histories

- Website analytics

- Social media engagement metrics

- Customer service logs

Look for patterns. Are there commonalities among your best customers? What about those who churned quickly? This data will form the foundation of your personas.

Step 3: Conduct Buyer Interviews

Now it's time to get direct input from your customers. Set up interviews with a diverse range of clients, focusing on those who represent your ideal customer.

Here are some key areas to cover in your interviews:

- **Role**: What's their job title? What does a typical day look like?

- **Company**: What industry do they work in? What's the size of their company?

- **Goals**: What are they trying to achieve in their role?

- **Challenges**: What obstacles stand in their way?

- **Information Sources**: Where do they go to learn about industry trends or solutions?

- **Decision-Making Process**: How do they evaluate and choose products or services like yours?

Remember, the goal isn't just to collect facts, but to understand their story. What motivates them? What keeps them up at night?

Step 4: Analyse Social Media

Your social media followers can provide a wealth of information for your buyer personas. They're people who have already shown interest in your brand or industry.

Look at the types of content that get the most engagement, the profiles of your most active followers, and the comments and questions people leave on your posts. This can give you insights into their interests, pain points, and how they interact with brands online.

Step 5: List Your Findings

Now it's time to bring all this information together. Look for common themes and patterns across your data sources. Start grouping similar characteristics together.

You might find that you have several distinct personas emerging. Fear not—that's okay! Most businesses have multiple buyer personas, each representing a different segment of their ideal customer base.

Step 6: Bring Your Personas to Life

This is where you turn your data into a narrative. Give each persona a name, a job title, and a brief backstory. But remember, this isn't creative writing. Every detail should be grounded in your research.

Include:

- Demographic information
- Career background
- Goals and challenges
- Preferred communication channels
- Decision-making factors

Step 7: Implement and Iterate

Creating your personas is just the beginning. The real value comes from using them in your day-to-day operations.

As we'll explore more in future chapters, **personas can guide content creation**. Every piece of content should speak directly to one or more of your personas. You may also want to reference them in sales meetings, as they can help your sales team tailor their approach to each prospect. Product development teams can benefit too, as your new-found personas can inform the features and benefits you prioritise.

Most importantly, don't let your personas stagnate. **Revisit them regularly—at least every six months**. Are they still accurate? Has new data or market change rendered some aspects obsolete? Be prepared to adjust and evolve your personas over time.

The Payoff from Well-Crafted Buyer Personas

Creating detailed, accurate buyer personas takes time and effort. But the payoff can be enormous.

When you truly understand your ideal customers:

- Your marketing messages resonate more deeply

- Your content attracts more qualified leads

- Your sales team can personalise their approach more effectively

- Your product development aligns more closely with customer needs

In short, well-crafted buyer personas turn your marketing from a scattergun approach into a laser-focused strategy.

Remember this: perfection is the enemy of progress. Your first attempt at creating personas won't be flawless, and that's okay.

The key is to start with the information you have, use these personas in your marketing efforts, and refine them based on the results you see. At the end of this chapter, you'll find a template that you can use.

Your buyer personas are the foundation upon which your entire marketing strategy will be built. Take the time to get them right, and you'll find that every other aspect of your marketing becomes more focused, more effective, and more aligned with the needs of your ideal customers.

In the next chapter, we'll explore the impact buyer personas can have on your wider marketing efforts. But for now, gather your team, dive into your data, and start bringing your buyer personas to life.

Your future marketing success depends on it.

_____ *Chapter Summary* _____

- Many businesses create superficial buyer personas that lack real-world grounding, focusing on fiction rather than facts.

- Effective persona creation requires input from multiple teams: marketing, sales, customer service, and product development.

- Building accurate personas involves analysing existing data, conducting customer interviews, and studying social media engagement.

- Personas must be living documents that guide daily decisions and be regularly updated to reflect changing customer needs.

- Well-crafted personas help focus marketing messages, attract qualified leads, and align product development with customer needs.

BUYER PERSONA

2 Psychographics

Values	Interest	Lifestyles	Goals and aspirations	Pain points and challenges

1 Demographics

Age

Location

Job title

Company

Demographic information

3 Professional Background

Career Background

Goals and Challenges

4 Behavioural & Buying Insights

Buying habits and preferences

Decision-making process

Decision-making factors

5 Communication Preferences

Preferred Communication Channels

Information Sources

CHAPTER 10

The Transformative Power of Buyer Personas on Your Strategy

As we explored in the previous chapter, buyer personas are not just marketing tools; they're the compass that guides your entire business.

But here's what most businesses miss: well-crafted buyer personas don't just reveal what your customers want. They uncover *why* they trust one solution over another.

When you truly understand your ideal customers, **you discover their specific trust triggers**—the proof points they need to see, the concerns that keep them awake at night, the past experiences that make them sceptical, and the values that must align before they'll hand over their money.

Think of it this way: every buyer has a unique "trust button."

Some people trust data and statistics.

Others trust personal recommendations.

Some need to see social proof from peers in their industry.

Others require extensive educational content before they feel confident in making their decision.

By understanding these trust preferences at the persona level, you can aim directly for each customer's trust button, rather than hoping your generic messaging will somehow resonate.

That's why, in this chapter, we're going to explore how these semi-fictional representations of your ideal customers can revolutionise not just your marketing, but your entire organisation, by helping you build trust more strategically and effectively.

The Ripple Effect: From Marketing to Business-Wide Impact

When you drop a stone in a pond, the ripples spread far beyond the initial point of impact.

Similarly, the influence of buyer personas extends far beyond your marketing department. Let's explore how these ripples transform various aspects of your business:

1. Marketing: Laser-Focused Precision

At its core, the impact of buyer personas on marketing boils down to one fundamental principle: **focus**.

With buyer personas at the helm, your marketing efforts transform from a scattergun approach to a precision instrument.

Consider this: according to HubSpot, using buyer personas can make your website between two and five times more effective and easier to use[2]. Why? Because every element, from your messaging to your design, is crafted with your ideal buyer in mind.

Let's break down the areas where this focus manifests:

- **Website content**: Your website becomes a mirror, reflecting the needs, desires, and pain points of your target audience. When visitors land on your site, they feel an immediate connection—as if you're speaking directly to them.

- **Blog posts and content**: Instead of creating content for "anyone and everyone," you're crafting pieces that address the specific questions and concerns of your buyer personas. This targeted approach not only attracts more qualified leads but also positions you as an authority in your niche.

- **Product and service promotion**: With a clear understanding of your ideal customers, you can tailor how you present your offerings. You're not just listing features; you're highlighting the benefits that matter most to your personas.

The results can be staggering. A case study by MarketingSherpa found that buyer personas increased website session length by 900% and the number of pages visited by 100%[3].

But the benefits don't stop at engagement. When it comes to organic search traffic, persona-crafted content can boost your numbers dramatically—sometimes by upwards of 50%.

Why? Because you're creating content that aligns perfectly with what your ideal customers are searching for.

Even your email marketing gets a boost. Rock Content[4] reported that click-through rates of persona-focused emails increased by 14%, with conversion rates jumping by 10%. When your emails speak directly to your readers' needs and interests, they're far more likely to take action.

2. Sales: Empathy-Driven Conversions

Now, let's follow those marketing-qualified leads as they make their way to your sales team. Here, buyer personas take on a new role: they become a tool for empathy and qualification.

Imagine your sales team armed with detailed profiles of your ideal customers. They're not just pushing a product—they're offering solutions to specific problems they know their prospects are facing.

According to ITSMA, buyers are 48% more likely to consider solution providers that personalise their marketing to address their specific business issues.[5]

But it's not just about closing deals. Buyer personas help your sales team in two crucial ways:

1. **Lead qualification**: By cross-referencing incoming leads with your buyer personas, your sales team can quickly identify which prospects are most likely to be a good fit. This isn't about dismissing potential customers; it's about focusing your team's energy where it's most likely to yield results.

2. **Empathetic selling**: When your sales team understands the pain points, goals, and challenges of your buyer personas, they can approach conversations with genuine empathy. They're not just reciting features—they're discussing how your solution addresses the specific issues your prospect is facing.

3. Customer Support and Onboarding: Personalised Experiences

The journey doesn't end when a lead becomes a customer. Your buyer personas continue to add value throughout the customer lifecycle, particularly in support and onboarding.

Think about it: your personas include information about the main problems your ideal customers are facing. Armed with this knowledge, your customer support and onboarding teams can:

- Anticipate common issues and proactively address them

- Tailor the onboarding process to address each customer's likely pain points

- Communicate in a way that resonates with each customer's preferences and background

The result? **A customer experience that feels personalised and attentive, leading to higher satisfaction and loyalty**.

The Real Reason Why Buyer Personas Work

At the heart of the buyer persona's effectiveness is the central theme of this entire book: trust. When every touchpoint of your business—from your website copy to your sales conversations to your customer support—feels tailored to the customer, it builds a deep sense of understanding and rapport.

Your potential customers aren't just interacting with a faceless business. Now, they're engaging with an organisation that seems to *get* them. This perceived understanding is the foundation of trust, and that will continue to develop as you work through the remaining chapters.

The bottom line is that buyer personas drive growth. The impact of well-crafted and well-implemented buyer personas on your business can be profound.

According to Marketer Insider Group, a staggering 93% of companies who exceed lead and revenue goals segment their database by buyer persona[6].

That statistic alone should be the call to action for you and your team. It suggests that mastering your buyer personas isn't just a marketing exercise, but also a key driver of business growth.

From Theory to Practice: Implementing Persona-Driven Strategies

Understanding the power of buyer personas is one thing. Harnessing that power is another.

Think about sharing personas across departments, ensuring every team—from marketing to sales to customer support—has access to them and understands how to use them.

You may also want to create a system for teams to provide feedback on the accuracy and usefulness of your personas. This information can help you refine and update your personas over time.

Your buyer personas are not set in stone. As your business grows and evolves, so too should your understanding of your ideal customers. Make it a habit to revisit and refine your personas regularly, ensuring they continue to drive your business forward.

Take a moment to consider: how well do you really know your ideal customers? And more importantly, how effectively are you using that knowledge to drive your business forward?

The answers to these questions could be the key to unlocking your next phase of growth.

_____ *Chapter Summary* _____

- Well-crafted buyer personas improve multiple areas: making websites more effective, focusing content creation, and boosting email engagement.

- Sales teams benefit through better lead qualification and more empathetic conversations based on deep customer understanding.

- Customer support and onboarding improve when teams can anticipate needs and tailor experiences to specific customer types.

- Success requires sharing personas across departments, providing regular training, and creating feedback loops to refine them over time.

- Companies exceeding their goals typically segment their database by buyer persona, demonstrating the business impact of proper implementation.

CHAPTER 11

Buyer Persona Workshop: Addressing Common Questions and Strategies

You've taken your first steps into the world of buyer personas, and like any journey into new territory, you're bound to have questions.

In this chapter, we'll address some of the most common queries and misconceptions that arise when crafting buyer personas.

Think of this as your buyer persona troubleshooting guide—a compass to keep you on track as you navigate this crucial aspect of your marketing strategy.

The Relevance Question: Do Buyer Personas Still Matter?

Let's start with the elephant in the room: are buyer personas still relevant?

To answer this, let's flip the question on its head:

1. Do you want your marketing to address the specific needs and pain points of your audience?

2. Do you want to communicate with your potential customers in an honest and transparent way?

If you answered "yes" to these questions (and I hope you did!), then you've answered your original question. Buyer personas are not just relevant; they're essential. **They provide the foundational platform for targeting content specifically to the audience you want to reach**.

Think of buyer personas as the architectural blueprints for your marketing strategy. Just as you wouldn't build a house without a plan, you shouldn't construct your marketing efforts without a clear picture of who you're building them for.

The Niche Question: Should I Use Buyer Personas to Identify a Niche?

Dan Tyre, an executive at HubSpot, once said, "The riches are in the niches." This, for me, encapsulates a profound truth about modern business: specialisation often leads to greater success.

Whether you're considering niching down by sector, service, software, or even personal qualities, your buyer personas can be an invaluable guide. Remember, **your personas represent the archetype of who you want to work with**.

However, I would always advise caution in this scenario. While your personas can help identify potential niches, they shouldn't be the only factor in your decision. Consider market size, competition, and your own expertise and passion when choosing a niche.

The Naming Question: To Name or Not to Name?

It's a common practice to give buyer personas alliterative names like "Brian the Business Owner" or "Helen the HR Manager."

It sounds catchy, doesn't it? But here's a word of caution: naming your personas can introduce unintended bias into your marketing efforts.

Even if you use a fictional name, you're potentially creating a very specific image in your mind of your best-fit customer. This can lead to two problems:

1. You might unconsciously seek out customers who fit this narrow image, potentially missing out on other great prospects.

2. You might hesitate to convert leads who don't fit this image, even if they're a good fit for your product or service.

Let's consider an example. Imagine you describe a persona as "male, raised in the UK, lives in a castle, and is significantly wealthy." You might be thinking of His Majesty King Charles III. But couldn't this also describe Ozzy Osbourne? By naming and overly specifying your persona, you risk discounting potential customers who don't fit your narrow mental image.

The solution? Keep it simple and unbiased. Instead of names, use titles like "Business Owner Persona A" or "HR Manager Persona B." This approach keeps your focus on the role and needs of your ideal customer, rather than on superficial characteristics.

The Photo Fallacy: Should I Include a Picture?

While we're on the subject of bias, let's talk about photos. **Many buyer persona templates include a stock photo on the first page**. But just like naming, this can introduce racial, gender or even beauty bias into your marketing.

For instance, if your "Alice the Accountant" persona features a picture of a young, white female, you might unconsciously strive to attract only leads that fit that profile. This not only limits your potential customer base but also risks misrepresenting your actual audience.

So instead, **skip the photo altogether**. A picture might be worth a thousand words, but in this case, those words might be leading you astray. By omitting the photo, you'll create personas that are more representative of your diverse audience, allowing your product, messaging and communications to resonate more broadly.

The Detail Dilemma: How In-Depth Should My Personas Be?

When it comes to buyer personas, there's a common misconception that they should only detail character traits, demographics and socio-graphic information. But personas like this are fundamentally flawed because they don't tell you why and how someone will want to buy your product or service.

A well-crafted buyer persona is like a high-resolution photograph—the more detail it contains, the clearer the picture. Your personas should include:

- Demographics (age, location, job title)

- Psychographics (values, interests, lifestyle)

- Pain points and challenges

- Goals and aspirations

- Buying habits and preferences

- Decision-making process

Remember, the goal isn't just to describe your ideal customer, but to understand them. **Your personas should provide insight into what motivates your customers, what problems they're trying to solve, and how your product or service fits into their lives**.

The Negative Persona: Do I Need One?

While buyer personas help you identify who you want to work with, **it can be equally valuable to identify who you don't want as a customer**. Enter the negative buyer persona.

According to Mark W. Schaefer[7], 3-4 personas often account for over 90% of a company's sales. But for most businesses, there will be people who are not a good fit—they might not align with your niche, or they might be challenging clients who cause more frustration than profit.

Creating a negative buyer persona can help you:

1. Avoid wasting resources on marketing to the wrong audience

2. Improve the efficiency of your sales process by quickly identifying poor-fit leads

3. Refine your messaging to better attract your ideal customers

Think of a negative persona as a "No Entry" sign on your marketing roadmap. It helps you steer clear of dead ends and keeps you focused on the path to your ideal customers.

The Content Connection: How Do Personas Help My Content Strategy?

If you're wondering how buyer personas tie into your content strategy, you're asking the right question. In fact, this connection is so crucial that it forms the next step in The Trust BLUEPRINT™.

For now, think of your buyer personas as the foundation upon which you'll build your content strategy. They inform:

- What topics you should cover

- What tone and style to use

- Which channels to focus on

- How to structure your content for maximum impact

Just as a tailor needs precise measurements to create a perfect fit, your content strategy needs detailed buyer personas to create content that resonates with your audience.

Putting It All Together: Your Buyer Persona Action Plan

Now that we've addressed these common questions and misconceptions, let's recap with a practical action plan:

- **Reassess your current personas**: Look at your existing personas (if you have them) with fresh eyes. Are they detailed enough? Are they free from unintended bias?

- **Ditch the names and photos**: If you're using names or stock photos for your personas, consider removing them to reduce bias.

- **Deepen your persona details**: Ensure your personas go beyond basic demographics. Include psychographics, pain points and buying behaviours.

- **Consider creating a negative persona**: Identify the characteristics of customers you don't want to target.

- **Align your team**: Share your refined personas across all departments and ensure everyone understands how to use them.

- **Plan for regular reviews**: Set a schedule to review and update your personas regularly—markets and customers evolve, and your personas should too.

- **Prepare for content creation**: As you refine your personas, start thinking about how they will inform your content strategy.

Remember, creating effective buyer personas is an ongoing process of refinement and application. Each iteration brings you closer to a deeper understanding of your ideal customers, setting the stage for more targeted, effective marketing.

In the next section of The Trust BLUEPRINT™, we'll dive into how to leverage these carefully crafted personas in your content strategy. You've laid the foundation, now it's time to start building.

Chapter Summary

- Buyer personas remain essential for targeted marketing but should avoid bias from overly specific names or photos.

- Effective personas need depth beyond basic demographics, including motivations, challenges and decision-making processes.

- Negative personas help identify poor-fit customers and prevent wasted resources on the wrong audiences.

- Keep personas practical and bias-free by focusing on roles and needs rather than superficial characteristics.

- Regular review and refinement of personas ensures they evolve with changing markets and customer needs.

CHAPTER 12

BLUEPRINT Step 2: Learning - Becoming Your Industry's Best Teacher

"I don't want to give away our secrets."

If I had a pound for every time I've heard that phrase, I'd be writing this book from a private island. But here's the thing: **there are no secrets, only companies that choose to be helpful and those that don't**.

In retrospect, writing that line sounds like something a Bond villain might say, but it holds true for every buying decision you make.

Think about the last time you made a major purchase. Before you even thought about contacting a company, you probably did your research online. Remember, according to Google's Zero Moment of Truth, 80% of the buying decision is made before a prospect first reaches out.

In the previous step, we explored how to understand your ideal customer. Now it's time to become their trusted teacher.

Picture this: your potential customer is searching for answers at 2 a.m. They have questions, concerns and doubts. Who's going to help them? The company that hides behind vague promises, or the one that answers their questions honestly and completely?

In the upcoming chapters, we'll explore why education is the new marketing. You'll see a real-life example from one man who saved his pool company by obsessing over customer questions, why addressing problems head-on can generate millions in revenue, and how creating a comprehensive Learning Hub can transform your business.

We'll tackle the "Big 5" topics that drive every purchase decision, show you how to turn your website into a lead-generating education centre, and demonstrate why the companies that teach best, sell best.

Think of it as turning your marketing from a megaphone into a classroom. Because in a world where buyers are more informed than ever, **when you truly teach, trust naturally follows**.

CHAPTER 13

We Are All Educators: Harnessing the Power of Inquiry and Knowledge

We will all have made a significant purchase at some point in our lives: a car, a house, an engagement ring.

Before you even think about reaching out to a company, what's the first thing you do?

You dive into research mode.

You scour the internet, read reviews and compare options.

This crucial phase of the buyer's journey is the Zero Moment of Truth, and it is reshaping the way businesses need to approach marketing.

In Chapter 6, we talked about this: on average, 80% of the buying decision is made online before a prospect first contacts a business. Whether it's picking up the phone or filling out a form on a website, that lead is likely already 80% through the buying process. They're just looking for that final push.

The Simple (Yet Powerful) Solution

Now, you might be wondering, "What's the best way to build that trust?" The answer is so obvious you'll be left scratching your head wondering why you haven't done it sooner: obsess over answering your customers' questions.

"But it can't be that simple!" I hear you protesting, so let me show you by telling a story about a man who saved his business by doing just that.

Meet my good friend Marcus Sheridan, whose career started as a "pool guy" at River Pools and Spas in the USA. In the early 2000s, his business was thriving. If you wanted a pool, you could easily get a loan or borrow against your home equity.

Then came 2008 and the financial crash. On 10 October 2008, the Dow Jones plummeted nearly 500 points, ushering in the recession many of us remember all too well.

Within 48 hours, five of Marcus's customers who had put down deposits withdrew.

$250,000, gone in just two days.

By January 2009, Marcus and his team were on the brink. Three consultants advised him to file for bankruptcy. But for Marcus, that wasn't an option. It would mean losing not just his home, but his partners' homes too, and his team would be out of jobs.

The Power of Obsession (The Good Kind)

Faced with this dire situation, Marcus realised he needed to drive more traffic to his website, generate more leads, and ultimately build more trust. He turned to the internet, discovering concepts like inbound marketing and content marketing.

That's when a radical marketing principle dawned on him: **if he truly obsessed over the questions his buyers were asking, he might just save his business**.

If he was willing to listen to the questions asked every single day by prospects and customers, and address them on his website, he could turn things around.

And that's exactly what he did. He produced content that was honest and transparent, and he did it consistently.

This obsession with answering questions built trust with his audience and brought his company back from the brink.

Marketing tactics may have different names and processes, but fundamentally, the reason people buy from you is the same reason they buy from anyone else: **they trust you enough to part with their money**.

Trust is a principle that's not going away. To build it, we need to start by producing content that begins with obsessing over our buyers and addressing whatever they're thinking about.

Remember: if they're asking a question, they're searching for it online. The business that provides the answer is almost always the one that gets either their money or that first moment of truth—that first point of contact.

Your Marketing Roadmap

So, where do you start? Think like your buyer, not like a business. Ask yourself:

1. What fears do my buyers have?
2. What are the top questions my sales team receives?
3. Have I answered these questions with content on my website?

If not, you've found your starting point for content production. You can easily create 100+ blog article topics just from those questions above.

And this is just the beginning. In the next chapter, we'll dive even deeper into how you can harness the power of inquiry and knowledge to build unshakeable trust with your audience.

Remember, in the world of marketing, education is engagement. By obsessing over your customers' questions, you're not just providing information but building the foundation of a lasting, trust-based relationship.

_____ ***Chapter Summary*** _____

- Most buyers now complete 80% of their purchasing decisions through online research before making first contact.

- Trust is the fundamental principle that drives business success, regardless of industry or sector.

- Building trust starts with thoroughly answering customer questions through helpful online content.

- Marcus Sheridan's pool company story shows how focusing on answering customer questions can transform business results.

- Success requires thinking like your buyers and addressing their fears, concerns and questions transparently.

CHAPTER 14

Becoming an Educator: Embracing Honesty and Transparency in Content

When you're searching for information about a product you're considering buying, you have questions, concerns and a desire to compare options.

What if you found a company that answered all these queries openly and honestly, even if it meant admitting they're not the perfect fit for everyone?

Would you trust them more than the business that didn't?

This chapter explores the **Endless Customers System™, a powerful marketing approach that's transforming businesses worldwide**.

The Endless Customers System™ started as *They Ask, You Answer*, and is more than just a catchy phrase. It's a philosophy that saved Marcus Sheridan's pool company during the 2008 financial crisis and has since been adopted by businesses around the globe. At its core are these four pillars:

- Be willing to say what others in your industry avoid.

- Show what others in your space won't reveal.

- Sell in ways your competitors won't dare to try.

- Be more human in a way that others won't in your space.

These foundations underpin much of what we'll explore in this book. They're about building trust through radical honesty and transparency.

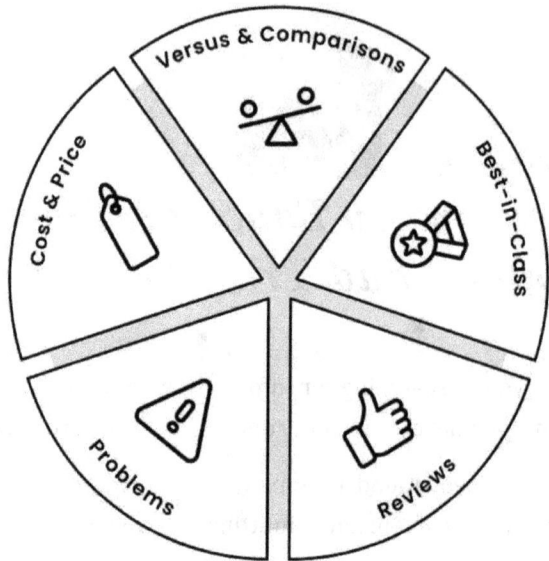

THE BIG 5

Versus & Comparisons

Cost & Price

Best-in-Class

Problems

Reviews

The 'Big 5': Content Topics That Drive Decisions

To truly craft content that meets your audience's needs, we need to focus on what is known as the 'Big 5'. These are five crucial content topics that influence buying decisions across every industry:

1. Cost and Price

2. Problems

3. Versus and Comparisons

4. Reviews

5. Best-in-Class

Let's dive into three of these (we'll tackle Cost and Price, and Problems in later chapters) and see how they can drastically impact your business.

1. Versus and Comparisons: Embracing the Competition

As buyers look for solutions, they often want to compare two or three options. **Many companies fear discussing their competition**, but here's a secret: your potential customers are already making these comparisons.

Why not guide them through the process?

The key is to be upfront and unbiased about the available options. Remember, you won't be the right fit for everyone, and pretending otherwise will only erode trust.

Marcus wrote a post comparing fiberglass to vinyl liner and concrete pools, admitting that the fiberglass pools he sells aren't right for everyone.

At no point did Marcus claim their product was better—because it simply isn't better for every situation.

His approach was rooted in transparency, because writing comparisons is only valid and effective when we're genuinely honest about the strengths and weaknesses of each option.

After publishing this post, he began ranking number one in search results for over a dozen comparison-related phrases. The trust built through this honesty led to higher conversion rates among readers who were genuinely good fits for his product.

2 & 3. Reviews and Best-in-Class: Turning Competitors into Traffic

Have you ever been in a meeting with a prospect when they ask: "We really like you and we're thinking of going with your company, but if we don't do business with you, is there someone else you'd recommend?"

Most companies would dodge this question or give a vague answer, fearing they'll lose the sale.

But this approach misses a crucial point: **if you're not honest, you're going to lose trust anyway.**

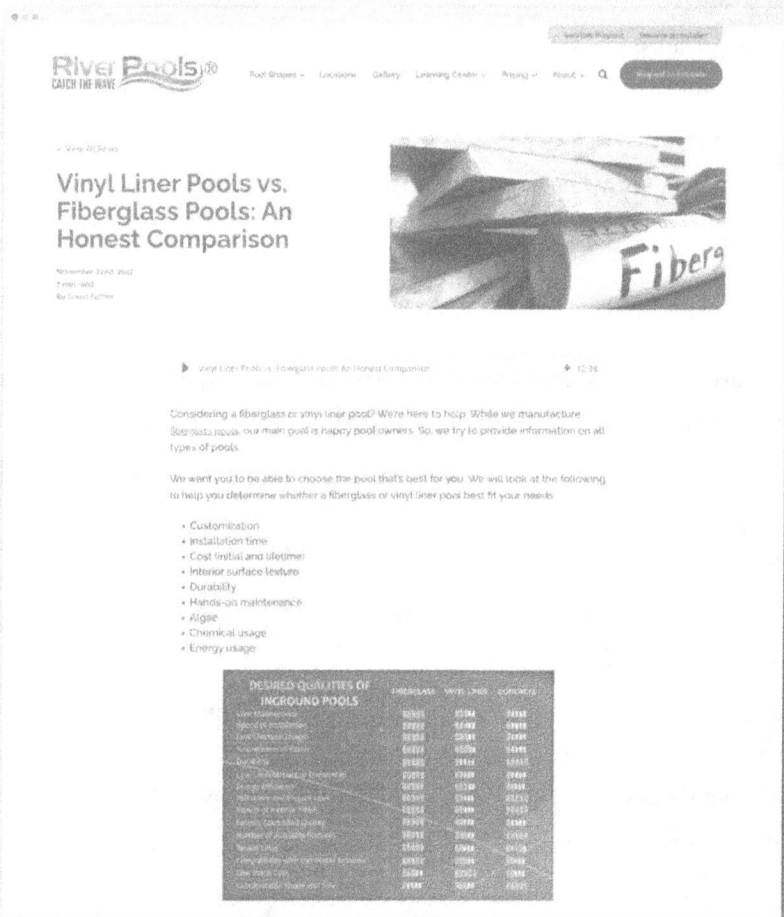

If you openly talk about your competition, you can build trust and capture traffic from them. At the same time, this approach offers a unique chance to demonstrate confidence in your offerings while establishing yourself as an honest broker of information.

Marcus put this theory to the test by writing an article titled *Who Are The Best Pool Builders in Richmond, Virginia? (Reviews/Ratings),* which included one of his competitors, Pla Mor Pools.

The result? When people searched for "reviews pla-mor pools richmond virginia", Marcus's article appeared as the top result, all because he created an honest review of his competitors.

But there's even another way to approach this: the Criteria-Based Best-in-Class List. This approach is particularly effective for ranking in AI-generated search results on platforms like Perplexity and ChatGPT.

In this scenario, **you create a best-in-class list that includes yourself among competitors, while teaching the market about important evaluation criteria**.

Shasta Pools demonstrated this brilliantly with their article *The Top 6 Pool Builders in Arizona in 2025*. They began with a bulleted list explaining the broad criteria that make a good pool builder, establishing themselves as educators rather than just salespeople.

At the same time, they listed themselves alongside several competitors and included detailed charts comparing each company against these criteria—an increasingly important trend in written content.

The results were astonishing. Very quickly, they found themselves being recommended by platforms like ChatGPT when users typed queries such as "who are the best pool builders in Arizona?"

This approach also works effectively for featured snippets and AI-generated content on Google. Roe Painting published *Compare the Best Concrete Coatings on the Market in 2025*, using a similar criteria-based approach.

They quickly saw Google referencing them in search queries for "best concrete coatings 2025" both as a featured snippet and in AI overview sections.

By focusing on educating rather than just promoting, these companies positioned themselves as authorities in their industries while simultaneously improving their visibility in both traditional and AI-powered search results.

The Informed Consumer: A New Reality

The power of the internet and the Zero Moment of Truth have transformed the consumer landscape.

For Marcus's business, River Pools and Spas, this strategy helped them grow from 2,000 to over 600,000 visitors a month, becoming the most trafficked pool website in the world.

Their story is one of many businesses embracing the Endless Customers System™. They are the businesses that recognise **the days of relying on consumer ignorance as a sales strategy are over**.

Today's consumers will find answers to their questions—the only question is, who will they fall in love with during their research process?

Will it be you? Or someone else?

By embracing honesty, addressing problems head-on, and providing comprehensive comparisons and reviews, you position yourself as a trusted educator in your field. This approach not only drives traffic but also builds the kind of trust that turns visitors into customers.

When you become an educator—honest, transparent and helpful— you're not just marketing. You're building relationships that can transform your business.

Chapter Summary

- The Endless Customers System™ builds trust through radical honesty about topics competitors avoid, focusing on the 'Big 5': Cost and Price, Problems, Comparisons, Reviews and Best-in-Class.

- When creating comparison content, never claim superiority. Be transparent about when your solution isn't the right fit, which builds credibility and attracts qualified leads.

- Honest recommendations about competitors demonstrate confidence and capture search traffic from those looking for competitor reviews.

- Criteria-based best-in-class content that includes yourself alongside competitors performs exceptionally well in both traditional search and AI-generated results.

- Consumers will find answers to their questions. Your choice is whether to be their trusted source or let them fall in love with someone else during their research.

CHAPTER 15

Guest Chapter: How Trust Saved My Business - A Journey from the Brink to Breakthrough

Like many business owners, I never set out to be in my industry. I was a college graduate with a young family, looking for an opportunity.

When my friends Jim Spiess and Jason Hughes asked me to help run their small pool retail store, I saw it as a temporary stepping stone. "I'll help you guys get going until I find out where I'll be working next," I told them.

Looking back, that statement makes me laugh.

Because what started as a temporary job became my passion. I threw myself into learning everything about pools. I studied. I read. I asked questions.

Within six months, I knew more about pools than my partners, and they offered me the chance to become a third owner in the business.

For years, business was good. The housing boom meant anyone could get a loan for a pool. We didn't have to be great marketers or salespeople—we just had to show up.

Then 2008 hit, and everything changed.

When I look back at March 2009, I still get chills thinking about how close we came to losing everything.

River Pools and Spas was on the brink of bankruptcy. Our bank account was overdrawn. Employees were sitting at home because we had no work. As a father and husband, I felt like I was failing my family.

Every night, I would make the same call to check our company's bank balance, hoping for a miracle. And every night, I'd hear that dreaded word: "Overdrawn."

Eventually, I started crying on my drives home, the weight of potential failure crushing me. This wasn't just about losing a business—it was about letting down my family, my employees, and their families too.

But in that darkness, I discovered something powerful. Something that would not only save my company but transform how I viewed business forever: **the simple principle that trust is everything.**

The Change

In that desperate moment, I started noticing something about my own buying behaviour. Whenever I needed information, I turned to Google. I was becoming my own salesperson, researching everything before making decisions.

And I realised something: our customers were doing the exact same thing.

That's when I started obsessing over one question: "What are our potential customers really asking about pools? What do they actually want to know before making this huge purchase?"

The answer was obvious. They wanted to know about costs, problems, comparisons between different types of pools, honest reviews, and what defined quality in our industry.

Yet no one in the pool industry was willing to address these topics openly online.

Why? Because like most businesses, pool companies were afraid.

Afraid of giving away "trade secrets."

Afraid of competitors seeing their prices.

Afraid of discussing problems that might scare customers away.

But I had a revelation: **consumer ignorance is no longer a viable business strategy**. People are going to find answers to their questions. The only question is: **who will they trust more?** The company willing to give them honest answers, or the one that hides from their questions?

So, we did something radical. We started answering every single question our customers asked—honestly and transparently—through articles and videos on our website. Nothing was off-limits.

I sat down at my kitchen table late one night and wrote down every question I'd been asked about fibreglass pools over the previous nine years. Within 30 minutes, I had over 100 questions. Then, working late into the night after my family was asleep, my partners and I began answering each one.

The results were astounding. Within months, our website traffic exploded. More importantly, the quality of our leads improved dramatically. They trusted us because we had educated them.

In 2009, we were getting about 20,000 visitors to our website per month. By 2020, we were averaging over 600,000 monthly visitors, making us the most trafficked swimming pool website in the world.

But here's what's interesting: the average River Pools customer now reads 105 pages of our website before making a purchase.

Think about that. *105 pages!*

When I tell this to business owners, they often say, "That's impossible. No one would read that much."

But they're wrong. When people are making important buying decisions, they will consume as much information as it takes to feel confident. And they'll buy from the company that helps them feel that confidence.

Our closing rates skyrocketed. Instead of needing 250 sales appointments to sell 75 pools, we now needed only 120 appointments to sell 95 pools. Why? Because by the time customers met with us, they already trusted us. We had answered all their questions honestly.

Beyond Pools: A Business Philosophy is Born

What started as a desperate attempt to save my pool company became something much bigger. I began speaking about our approach at conferences, and business owners from every industry imaginable approached me saying, "This could work for us too."

And it has. I've watched companies in healthcare, manufacturing, software, professional services, and countless other industries transform their businesses using these same principles.

Because at its core, the Endless Customers System™ isn't about pools, or content marketing, or even digital strategy.

It's about trust.

The Lesson for Every Business

The lesson I learned from nearly losing everything is this: you build trust by being radically transparent—by having the courage to answer the questions everyone else in your industry is afraid to address.

The companies that will thrive in the future aren't necessarily the biggest or the ones with the most resources. They're the ones willing to be the most helpful, the most transparent, the best teachers in their space.

Every industry has its elephants in the room—the topics everyone knows about but no one wants to discuss. The businesses willing to address these topics openly and honestly will win the trust of their marketplace.

My journey from struggling pool guy to helping businesses around the world embrace transparency has taught me that building trust isn't complicated.

It simply requires the courage to teach, to answer questions honestly, and to put your customers' needs first.

Trust saved my business. And I believe it can transform yours too.

But only if you're willing to embrace radical honesty and transparency.

Only if you're willing to answer the questions your customers are really asking, not just the ones you feel comfortable answering.

Because in the end, business isn't about protecting trade secrets or controlling the conversation.

It's about earning trust.

And trust is earned through honesty, transparency, and a genuine desire to help others make informed decisions.

That's the real secret to success.

And it's available to any business willing to embrace it.

- **Marcus Sheridan, Author, *Endless Customers***

Chapter Summary

- During the 2008 financial crisis, River Pools and Spas faced bankruptcy until they recognised customers were researching extensively online before making purchasing decisions.

- The business transformed by answering every customer question honestly through articles and videos, even addressing topics other pool companies avoided like costs, problems, and comparisons.

- Website traffic grew from 20,000 to 600,000 monthly visitors, making it the most visited swimming pool website globally, with customers reading an average of 105 pages before purchasing.

- Sales efficiency dramatically improved; they needed only 120 appointments to sell 95 pools compared to previously requiring 250 appointments to sell 75 pools.

- The key lesson: businesses that build trust through radical transparency and honest answers to difficult industry questions will win customer confidence regardless of company size or resources.

Reader's Resource: Inspired by Marcus Sheridan's story of transformation through trust?

Scan this QR code to get your copy of "Endless Customers" and discover how to apply these trust-building principles to your own business. Learn the complete Endless Customers System™ directly from the man who developed it.

CHAPTER 16

The Learning Hub: Creating Content That Draws Your Ideal Customer In

I love visiting bookshops, especially when I'm travelling. You walk in and see thousands of books, your eye catching a few based on the title and cover design. But you only leave with the ones that truly resonate with you.

Now, replace the bookshop with the internet and the books with digital content. This is the challenge businesses face today: not just attracting but retaining the attention of their ideal customers amidst a sea of digital information.

While blog content is crucial for building trust, many businesses stop there. But I have some bad news: most blogs... well, they're not great.

The problem is twofold:

- Blog content often only scratches the surface in addressing buyer pain points and helping them make purchasing decisions.

- Blogs are often not effective at capturing leads.

Yes, they can generate interest in your brand and attract leads to your website, but they often fall short of providing a tangible method of capturing those leads for you to convert into customers.

Enter the Learning Hub (or Knowledge Hub, Learning Centre, and so on; the principle is the same).

A Learning Hub is more than just "gated content" (content hidden behind a form). It's a central repository of valuable and relevant information.

This approach not only builds trust and credibility with your potential clients but can also position your business as a go-to resource for insights and knowledge, establishing you as the thought leader in your industry.

The Power of Downloadable Content

Downloadable content is a marketer's secret weapon for generating leads and nurturing prospects through the sales funnel.

When you "gate" your content behind a form, asking for details like name and email address, you're not only providing valuable information to your audience, but you're gaining valuable information in exchange.

This strategy allows you to:

- Build a qualified email list

- Create a database of your target audience

- Keep your products or services top of mind through email marketing

- Position your business as a thought leader

When prospects are ready to make a purchase decision, they're more likely to choose a company that has consistently provided them with valuable and relevant content.

Downloadable content serves as a valuable complement to the "Big 5" topics we discussed in Chapter 14. By offering in-depth resources related to these topics, you can further solidify your expertise and provide prospects with the information they need to make informed decisions.

For example, if one of your "Big 5" topics is "Sustainable Living," a downloadable guide on *10 Eco-Friendly Home Improvements* could be a valuable resource for potential customers interested in that subject.

Not only does it complement the "Big 5", but **downloadable content provides you with ample opportunities for lead generation**. By their very nature of being gated behind a form, you're able to gather contact information in exchange for the valuable content you are offering.

Taking that further, you can then use this contact information to nurture leads, something we will talk about later in Chapter 22. This allows you to educate prospects, build trust, and move them through the sales process more effectively.

Lastly, downloadable content is the perfect space to create thought leadership. **This is a prime platform for positioning your company and experts as industry authorities**.

Building a Buyer-Centric Learning Centre

To create a Learning Centre that truly serves your audience, here are a couple of steps you'll want to consider:

1. **Complement your blog posts**: Think about what content you can create that builds on the topics you're already writing about.

2. **Diversify your content types**: Consider eBooks, whitepapers, infographics, case studies, webinars, and product demos. These are all content types we'll explore in later chapters.

3. **Focus on customer outcomes**: Organise your content around audience needs, interests, and pain points, not just product features or service benefits.

4. **Enhance user experience**: Implement clear categorisation, search functionality, and related content suggestions.

5. **Leverage customer insights**: Engage with your customers through interviews and surveys to understand their motivations and preferences. Use this feedback to create content that resonates on both emotional and practical levels.

The Long Game of Content Creation

Creating a Learning Hub is a long-term strategy.

It won't deliver overnight results, but the compounding effects can be remarkable. Think of it as planting seeds in a garden. At first, you might not see much growth, but with consistent care and patience, you'll eventually have a thriving ecosystem that attracts your ideal customers.

Just as the right books in a bookshop draw the keen interest of specific readers, the right content in your digital Learning Hub will attract and retain your ideal customers.

By following these principles and committing to consistent improvement, **you can create a Learning Centre that provides valuable information, guides prospects towards informed purchase decisions, and fosters long-lasting relationships with your brand**.

A well-crafted Learning Hub isn't just a marketing tool, but a trust-building machine that can transform casual browsers into loyal customers.

_____ *Chapter Summary* _____

- A Learning Hub goes beyond basic blogging by providing in-depth downloadable resources that address buyer needs.

- Gated content allows businesses to build qualified email lists while positioning themselves as thought leaders.

- Effective Learning Hubs complement blog content and the "Big 5" topics with diverse content types organised around customer needs.

- Creating an effective Learning Hub requires enhancing user experience through clear categorisation and leveraging customer insights from interviews and surveys to develop resonant content.

- Building a comprehensive resource centre is a long-term strategy that compounds over time to attract and retain ideal customers.

CHAPTER 17

BLUEPRINT Step 3: Understanding - Peeling Back the Curtain

You might be scratching your head right now, thinking, "Wait a minute, didn't we just cover 'Learning'? How is 'Understanding' any different?"

Fair question, my friend. Let me break it down for you.

While 'Learning' is about soaking up information, **'Understanding' is about making sense of it all**. It's the difference between knowing the ingredients and baking the cake.

So far, we've established that your potential customer is googling like crazy, devouring every piece of content they can find. They're stuffed with information. But now, they're facing the big question: "Who do I actually want to work with?"

Maybe they're choosing an accountant they'll stick with for decades. Or perhaps they're a business looking for a marketing agency to be their creative better half for the foreseeable future.

This is where 'Understanding' comes in. **It's about helping your audience see what life would be like with you in their corner**. How do you operate? What's your secret sauce? What can they expect if they decide to tango with your business?

In the upcoming chapters, we're going to pull back the curtain and show you how to give your audience this deeper understanding.

We'll tackle the most unnecessarily controversial marketing topic of all time. Yes, we're going to be talking about pricing on your website.

So, buckle up! We're about to turn your potential customers' knowledge into true understanding, transforming them from casual browsers into confident buyers.

CHAPTER 18

Operational Transparency: Unveiling the Magic Behind the Curtain

Who doesn't love watching a master chef at work? You sit at the counter of an open kitchen, watching them select ingredients, explain their techniques, and carefully craft each dish.

They tell you why they're using a particular spice, how the temperature affects the texture, and what they're looking for as they taste and adjust.

When your meal arrives, it's both delicious and fascinating. You appreciate the skill, the knowledge, and the care that went into every decision.

Compare that to eating at a restaurant where your food simply appears from a hidden kitchen. It might taste just as good, but you have no connection to the process, no understanding of the craft, and no appreciation for the expertise involved.

That's the power of operational transparency in business. When you show customers how you work, rather than hiding behind closed doors, you transform their relationship with your company from transactional to appreciative.

As a business, every move you make is constantly scrutinised by your audience. Like a tightrope walker balancing precariously above a breathless crowd, you can't hide your challenges or take shortcuts. Your process is on display, whether you like it or not.

But here's the kicker: that visibility isn't a weakness. No, it's your greatest strength—and more so, an opportunity.

Operational transparency transforms your relationship with customers. It's like inviting them backstage, showing them the gears and levers that make your business tick. It's saying: "Here's how we do what we do, warts and all."

Why does this matter? Because it gives your customers a crystal-clear picture of what a relationship with you looks like. No smoke and mirrors, just honest, open communication.

One easy way to do this is with a *How We Work* page on your website. This is your opportunity to show potential customers what a relationship with you looks like from their perspective.

Yes, you can still talk about your company values but frame them in terms of how they benefit the customer. Describe your onboarding process but focus on the customer's journey—not your internal checklist.

Remember, it's about addressing the elephant in the room. **No one wants to enter a business relationship blindfolded**. By openly discussing what working together looks like, you're building trust before the first handshake.

From "We" to "You": The Customer-Centric Shift

Let's shine a light on a common blind spot in business communication: the "we" syndrome.

You've seen it everywhere—websites plastered with "We do this, we offer that, we've won these awards."

It's a veil that obscures what truly matters to your customers.

The hard truth? Your customers aren't visiting your website for your life story. They're there because **they have a problem to solve**, and they're wondering if you're the right person to help them solve it.

When you lift the veil of "we-focused" language, you practise a powerful form of transparency. You stop hiding behind corporate achievements and start addressing what customers actually want to know: "What will my experience be like? Who exactly will I work with? How often will we communicate?"

This shift creates honest communication that reveals rather than conceals. It's transparency in its most practical form—**showing customers you understand their perspective rather than asking them to understand yours**.

When you stop talking about yourself and start framing everything through the customer's eyes, you're not just being customer-centric—you're being transparent about what truly matters in the relationship.

The most successful businesses aren't those that trumpet their own excellence. They're the ones brave enough to speak directly to their customers' needs, openly discussing how their services translate to customer outcomes. This is transparency that builds genuine connections, not just transactions.

Transparency isn't just a fancy buzzword to throw around in marketing meetings. It's a foundational business practice that aligns closely with honesty, trust, and client loyalty.

When clients understand what goes into delivering your service, they're more likely to value it. They see the effort, the expertise, the attention to detail. Suddenly, your pricing makes sense. Your timelines are understandable. Your processes are appreciated.

But the benefits don't stop at customer perception. Operational transparency forces you to take a hard look at your internal practices. Are they truly aligned with customer needs and expectations? If not, it's time for a change.

The Cost of Doing Business

And while we're pulling back the curtain, let's talk about the ultimate taboo: cost and price.

Yes, it's unconventional.

Yes, it's scary—so much so that I'm dedicating another two chapters after this one to write about it!

But being open about your pricing structure can be the final piece in your transparency puzzle.

By explaining the factors that influence your pricing, you're not just justifying your rates. You're educating your customers, helping them understand the value they're receiving. It's a bold move, but one that can set you apart in a sea of vague quotes and hidden fees.

Your Transparency Challenge

As we wrap up this chapter, I want to leave you with a challenge. Take a hard look at your business processes. Where can you inject more transparency? How can you shift your communication from "we" to "you"?

Operational transparency isn't about exposing every detail of your business. It's about **sharing the right information in the right way to build trust, demonstrate value, and create lasting relationships** with your customers.

Transparency isn't just nice to have. It's a competitive advantage.

_____ *Chapter Summary* _____

- Like watching a master chef, showing customers how your business works builds deeper appreciation and trust.

- Shift from "we-focused" language to transparent communication that reveals what truly matters to customers—their experience with you.

- Create detailed "How We Work" content that shows potential customers exactly what a relationship with you looks like.

- Being transparent about processes and pricing helps customers understand your value and builds trust before first contact.

- Operational transparency requires reviewing internal practices to ensure they truly align with customer needs.

CHAPTER 19

The Price Tag Taboo: Why Hiding Costs is Losing You Customers

How would you feel if you walked into a restaurant where the menu had no prices?

You're seated, ready to enjoy a meal, but there's a nagging worry in the back of your mind: "How much is this going to cost me?" Suddenly, your appetite for that juicy steak is overshadowed by financial anxiety. Your enjoyment of the meal is compromised before you've even taken a bite.

This scenario might seem absurd for a restaurant, yet it's precisely what many businesses do online every day. They hide their prices, **leaving potential customers in a state of confusion and frustration**.

In this chapter, we're going to shatter the price tag taboo and explore why transparency in pricing isn't just good ethics, it's good business.

The 10-Second Window of Opportunity

Let's start with a sobering statistic: You have 10 seconds.

That's it.

Ten measly seconds before a potential customer leaves your website if they can't find what they're looking for. And often, what they're looking for is price.

Think back to the last time you were genuinely excited to buy something. Did you make that purchase without knowing how much it cost? It's like playing a game where you don't know the rules —frustrating and ultimately pointless.

Attention is a precious commodity. If you can't capture and hold that attention quickly, you've lost a potential customer, possibly forever.

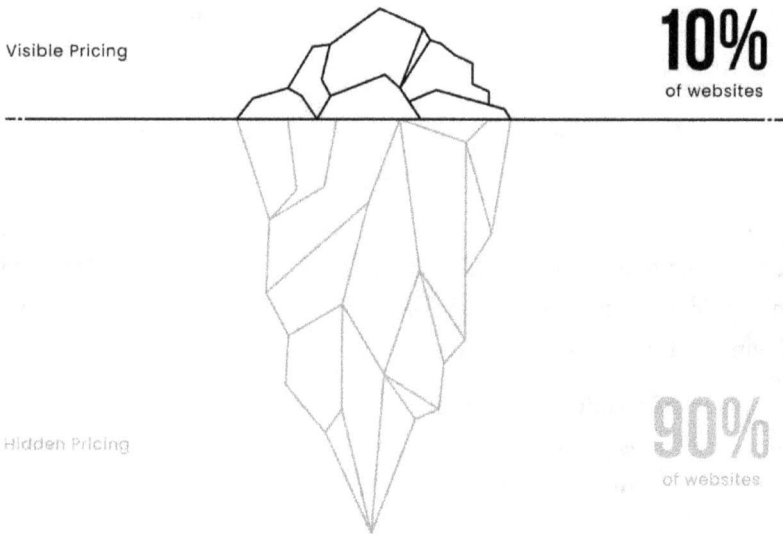

Visible Pricing

10%
of websites

Hidden Pricing

90%
of websites

The Price of Silence

Here's another shocking truth: **fewer than 10% of businesses worldwide address price on their website**.

That's right—90% of companies are willingly driving away potential customers by keeping quiet about their costs.

This silence is perhaps one of the biggest trust killers there is. When you refuse to discuss price, you're sending a clear message to your potential customers: "We don't trust you with this information."

And guess what? They'll return the favour by not trusting you.

But why? Why are so many businesses clinging to this outdated practice of price secrecy? The excuses are plentiful:

- "Our pricing is complicated."

- "We don't want our competitors to know our prices."

- "We're more expensive than others, and we don't want to scare people away."

So, let's tackle these one by one, shall we?

The "It's Complicated" Cop-Out

Yes, your pricing might be complex.

But you know what's more complex? Trying to guess what something costs with zero information. If your pricing depends on various factors, explain those factors. Show your audience what drives costs up or down. Give them a range. Anything is better than nothing.

Consider this: **if you can explain your pricing to a potential customer over the phone or in a meeting, you can explain it on your website.** The key is to break it down into digestible pieces. Use infographics, bullet points, or even interactive tools to help visitors understand your pricing structure.

Remember, complexity isn't a barrier to transparency. Instead, think of it as an opportunity to educate your audience and demonstrate your expertise.

The Competition Conundrum

News flash: **your competitors already have a pretty good idea of what you charge. And you probably have a ballpark figure for their prices too.** So why are we more worried about our competitors (who don't pay our bills) than our potential customers (who do)?

This fear of competitors knowing your prices is often overblown. In most industries, **pricing isn't the sole differentiator**. Your unique value proposition, quality of service, and customer experience play crucial roles in winning business.

Moreover, by being transparent about your pricing, you're positioning yourself as a leader in your industry. You're the one setting the standard for openness and honesty. That's a powerful differentiator.

The "We're Expensive" Excuse

Here's an ironic truth: buyers aren't scared when a company talks about price. They're terrified when a company hides it.

If you're more expensive, own it.

Explain why.

Show the value.

Trust your customers to make informed decisions.

Price isn't just a number; it's a reflection of value. If your prices are higher than average, use your website to justify that premium. Highlight your superior quality, exceptional service, or unique features. Help potential customers understand why you're worth every penny.

Remember, there will always be customers who prioritise quality over price. By being upfront about your costs, you're attracting the right kind of customers — those who value what you offer and are willing to pay for it.

The $45 Million Article

Still not convinced?

Let's go back to our friend Marcus Sheridan and River Pools and Spas.

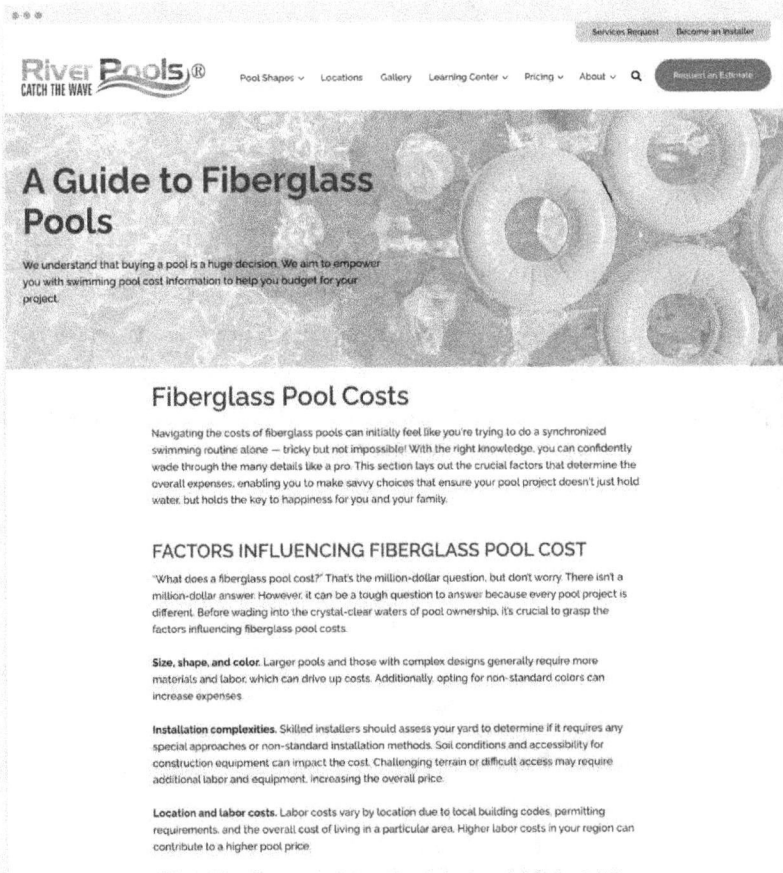

In 2009, during the recession, Marcus published an article titled *A Guide to Fibreglass Pool Costs*. It was a simple piece that explained what factors influence pool prices.

The result? **Within 48 hours, they were ranking number one on Google for 10 different search terms related to pool pricing**. But here's the kicker: over three years, that single article led to 708 customers and $45 million in revenue.

One article.

$45 million.

Let that sink in.

This isn't just a feel-good story; it's a testament to the power of pricing transparency. By addressing something that so many businesses shy away from, Marcus positioned his company as a trusted resource. He answered the questions that his competitors were too afraid to tackle.

But the benefits went beyond just attracting customers. This transparency also helped River Pools and Spas qualify leads more effectively. People who reached out after reading the article were already informed about pricing. They were serious buyers, not just tyre-kickers.

The Psychology of Pricing Transparency

To understand why pricing transparency is so powerful, we need to delve into a bit of psychology. When a company is open about its pricing, several positive effects occur:

- **Reduced uncertainty**: Humans are naturally averse to uncertainty. By providing clear pricing information, you're removing a significant source of stress for potential customers.

- **Increased trust**: Transparency signals honesty and confidence. When you're open about your prices, customers are more likely to trust you in other areas of your business as well.

- **Perceived control**: When customers have pricing information, they feel more in control of their decision-making process. This sense of control often leads to higher satisfaction, even if they end up paying more.

- **Anchoring effect**: By being the first to present a price, you set the anchor point against which all other options are judged. This can work in your favour, especially if you offer tiered pricing options.

- **Reduced post-purchase dissonance**: When customers know the price upfront, they're less likely to experience buyer's remorse later. They've had time to rationalise the cost before making a purchase.

Getting Started with "Cost and Price" Content

Now that you've read this chapter, I ask you: can you talk more about price?

Can you be the 10% that dares to be transparent?

Because if you don't earn your customers' trust by being open about pricing, someone else will.

Remember, consumer ignorance is no longer a viable strategy. Your potential customers are smart, impatient, and have the entire internet at their fingertips. They will find pricing information somewhere. Wouldn't you rather they get it from you?

This challenge isn't just about slapping a price list on your website. It's about fundamentally changing how you think about pricing in your marketing strategy. It's about viewing price not as a secret to be guarded, but as a tool for building trust and qualifying leads.

If you're ready to break the price tag taboo, start by auditing your website and determining how easy it is to find pricing information. When you're ready to create the content that explains your pricing structure, here are some practical steps:

1. **Explain the variables**: If your pricing is complex, break down what factors influence it. Create content that educates your audience on these variables. Consider creating a pricing calculator that allows visitors to estimate costs based on their specific needs.

2. **Provide ranges**: Even if you can't give exact figures, provide price ranges. It's better than leaving customers completely in the dark. Be sure to explain what might push a project to the lower or higher end of the range.

3. **Own your value**: If you're more expensive, explain why. Highlight the quality, service, or unique benefits that justify your pricing. Create comparison charts that show how your offering stacks up against cheaper alternatives.

4. **Create a pricing guide**: Take a page from Marcus's book and create comprehensive content about pricing in your industry. Be the go-to resource for pricing information. This could be a downloadable PDF, a series of blog posts, or even a video series.

5. **Be upfront about consultations**: If you need to provide custom quotes, say so clearly. But also give an idea of what range those quotes might fall into. Explain your quoting process so potential clients know what to expect.

6. **Use social proof**: Include testimonials or case studies that speak to the value customers have received. This helps justify your pricing and shows the real-world impact of your products or services.

7. **Address objections proactively**: Anticipate and address common objections to your pricing. This could be in the form of an FAQ section on your pricing page.

8. **Offer options**: If possible, provide different pricing tiers or packages. This gives customers choice and helps them find an option that fits their budget.

The Transparency Payoff

Embracing pricing transparency is not only an ethical practice, but also one that generates huge results. When you're open about costs:

- You build trust with potential customers

- You save time by pre-qualifying leads

- You differentiate yourself from competitors who are still hiding behind vague promises

- You become a valuable resource in your industry

- You attract customers who value quality and are less likely to haggle over price

- You reduce the sales cycle by addressing price concerns upfront

- You increase customer satisfaction by setting clear expectations from the start

In other words, secrecy doesn't protect you; it isolates you. Your prices aren't a shameful secret to be hidden away. They reflect your value, your quality, and your confidence in what you offer.

Overcoming Internal Resistance

Implementing pricing transparency isn't always easy. You might face resistance within your own organisation. Here are some common objections and how to address them:

- **"We'll lose our competitive advantage"**: Remind sceptics that your competitive advantage should come from your quality, service, and unique value proposition, not from hiding information.

- **"Our sales team won't have anything to negotiate with"**: Shift the focus from price negotiation to value demonstration. Transparent pricing allows sales teams to focus on explaining value rather than haggling.

- **"We'll scare away potential customers"**: Emphasise that you'll be attracting more qualified leads. It's better to have fewer, higher-quality leads than a flood of tyre-kickers.

- **"Our prices might change"**: Implement a system for regularly updating your pricing information. Be clear about when and why prices might change.

The Future of Pricing: Dynamic Transparency

As we look to the future, the trend towards pricing transparency is only going to grow. We are already seeing the emergence of dynamic pricing models in industries like air travel and ridesharing. These models adjust prices in real time based on demand and other factors.

But perhaps the most exciting development is the rise of self-selection tools—particularly pricing calculators. These interactive tools answer the question every buyer desperately wants to know: "How much is it?"

Think about it. **A pricing calculator puts control directly in your customers' hands**. They can adjust variables, add or remove features, and watch in real time as the price changes. It's transparency at its most engaging and empowering.

But more importantly, your potential customer, during this experience, is mentally trying on your product or service. They're imagining themselves as your customer.

The beauty of a pricing calculator is that it acknowledges the complexity of your pricing without using that complexity as an excuse for secrecy. It says, "Yes, our pricing depends on multiple factors—and we trust you enough to show you exactly how those factors work."

That's powerful stuff.

Companies that implement these tools see remarkable results:

- Shorter sales cycles (customers come pre-educated about price)
- Higher conversion rates (the mystery and anxiety are removed)
- Fewer tyre-kickers wasting your sales team's time
- More qualified leads who understand your value proposition

While this level of dynamic, interactive pricing might seem daunting at first, the underlying principle of transparency is universal. **The companies**

that will thrive in the future are those that embrace openness, not just in pricing, but in all aspects of their operations.

Your Next Steps

In a world where customers can find almost any information with a few clicks, trying to hide your prices is not only futile but counterproductive.

Remember, **pricing transparency is not just a marketing tactic—it's a business philosophy.**

It's about respecting your customers' time and intelligence.

It's about building trust from the very first interaction.

Trust me, your customers (and your bottom line) will thank you for it. The price of secrecy is too high in today's market. It's time to embrace transparency and reap the rewards of open, honest communication with your customers.

Are you ready to join the pricing transparency revolution?

Chapter Summary

- Less than 10% of businesses discuss pricing on their websites, despite price being a crucial factor in customer decision-making.

- Common excuses for hiding prices—complexity, competition, higher costs—ultimately harm trust and drive away potential customers.

- Being transparent about pricing builds trust, pre-qualifies leads, and can dramatically increase revenue, as shown by the $45 million pool pricing article.

- Effective price transparency includes explaining variables, providing ranges, justifying value, and offering self-selection tools like pricing calculators that empower customers.

- Success requires shifting the company mindset from seeing price as a secret to viewing it as a tool for building trust and qualifying leads.

CHAPTER 20

The Price is Wrong: Avoiding Common Pitfalls in Website Pricing Discussions

You've finally decided to take the plunge.

After reading the last chapter, you're ready to embrace pricing transparency on your website. You're excited, motivated, and ready to revolutionise how you communicate with potential customers.

But hold on a second, cowboy. Before you start throwing numbers around like confetti, let's talk about how to do this right.

Because here's the thing: **talking about price on your website isn't just about slapping a number on a page and calling it a day**. It's a delicate dance between information and persuasion, and like any dance, there are plenty of opportunities to step on your own toes.

In this chapter, we're going to explore the five most common mistakes businesses make when discussing cost and price on their websites.

Mistake #1: The "Me, Me, Me" Monologue

Imagine you're at a party, and you meet someone new.

They introduce themselves and then proceed to talk about nothing but themselves for the next hour—their achievements, their possessions, their opinions. How quickly would you be looking for the nearest exit?

Now, replace that self-absorbed partygoer with your website, and you've got the first common mistake: **not talking enough about the industry and marketplace**.

Here's a golden rule to tattoo on your forehead (or at least stick on a Post-it note on your computer screen): **80% of your pricing content should be about the marketplace. Only 20% should be about you**.

Why? Because context is king. Your potential customers don't just want to know your prices; they want to understand how those prices fit into the bigger picture. They're asking questions like:

- Is this price normal for the industry?

- What factors influence pricing in this market?

- How do economic trends affect costs in this sector?

By providing this context, you're not just giving a number; you're giving an education. You're positioning yourself as an expert in your field, someone who understands the nuances of the market.

So, how do you strike this 80/20 balance? Here are a few ideas:

- **Industry overview:** Provide a brief explanation of pricing trends in your industry.

- **Market factors:** Discuss external factors that influence pricing (e.g. raw material costs, regulatory changes).

- **Competitor analysis:** Without naming names, give an overview of different pricing models in your market.

- **Economic impact:** Explain how broader economic trends might affect pricing in your industry.

Your goal is to be a helpful industry insider. Give your potential customers the information they need to make an informed decision, and they'll thank you for it—possibly with their wallets.

Mistake #2: Hide and Seek with Your Pricing Page

The second common mistake is not including "Pricing" as a part of your navigation bar.

Remember our 10-second rule from the last chapter? Your potential customers are impatient. If they can't find your pricing information quickly and easily, they're going to assume one of two things:

1. You don't have any pricing information (strike one against transparency).

2. You're intentionally hiding it (strike two, three, and you're out).

The solution? **Put "Pricing" right there in your main navigation bar**, where it's impossible to miss.

This sends a message to your audience. By prominently displaying your pricing link, you're saying, "We have nothing to hide. We're confident in our pricing, and we respect your time too much to make you hunt for this information."

But wait, I hear you cry—won't this scare away potential customers? Won't they see the prices and run for the hills?

Not so fast. Remember, the goal isn't to get every single website visitor to become a customer. **The goal is to attract the right customers**—those who value what you offer and are willing to pay for it.

By being upfront about your pricing, you're qualifying leads before they even contact you. You're saving both your time and theirs.

So, go ahead. Put that "Pricing" link right up there in your main navigation.

Be bold.

Be transparent.

Be the company that respects its potential customers enough to give them the information they need right from the start.

Mistake #3: The Bait-and-Switch Pricing Page

When I was planning my wedding, we looked at a lot of venues and vendors.

The biggest frustration I found was one that is rife in all industries and business types. And it looks like this: you click on the *Pricing* page, excited to see if it fits your budget. But instead of clear, concrete information, you're met with vague phrases like "Competitive Pricing" or "Call for Quote".

Frustrating, isn't it?

Welcome to the third common mistake: being too generic with your pricing information, essentially creating a "bait-and-switch" page.

Now, I know what you're thinking. "But Tom, our pricing is complex! It depends on so many factors! We can't possibly give an exact price upfront!"

I hear you. Really, I do.

But here's the thing: your potential customers aren't asking for an exact, to-the-penny quote for their specific situation. They're looking for ballpark figures, ranges, or starting points. They want something—anything—to help them understand if you're in their league.

So, how do you provide meaningful pricing information without committing to a one-size-fits-all price? Here are a few ideas:

- **Price ranges:** Instead of a single price, provide a range. "Our services typically cost between £X and £Y, depending on [list factors]."

- **Starting prices:** If you can't give a range, at least give a starting point. "Prices start at £X."

- **Pricing tiers:** If you offer different levels of service, create clear tiers with pricing for each.

- **Pricing calculators:** For more complex products or services, consider creating an interactive pricing calculator that allows users to estimate costs based on their specific needs.

- **Sample quotes:** Provide examples of what a typical project or purchase might cost, along with details about what's included.

The goal is to give your potential customers enough information to determine if you're a good fit for their budget. By providing this information upfront, you're not just being transparent—you're also saving yourself from wasting time on leads that were never going to convert.

Mistake #4: The Jargon Jungle

Finally, we come to the fourth common mistake: assuming your audience knows what you're talking about when you refer to options, features, or industry-specific terms.

It's an easy trap to fall into.

You live and breathe your industry every day. Terms that seem basic to you might as well be ancient Greek to your potential customers.

And when people don't understand something, they tend to do one of two things: feel stupid (not a great emotion to associate with your brand) or leave (not what we want).

So, how do you avoid turning your pricing page into a jargon jungle? Here are a few tips:

- **Use plain language**: explain things as if you're talking to a smart friend who's not in your industry.

- **Define terms**: if you must use industry-specific terms, provide clear, concise definitions.

- **Provide context**: don't just list features; explain why they matter and how they benefit the customer.

- **Use visuals**: sometimes, a picture or an infographic really is worth a thousand words.

- **Offer examples**: illustrate complex concepts with real-world examples or case studies.

You want to educate, not intimidate. The more your potential customers understand about what they're paying for, the more comfortable they'll be with your pricing.

Mistake #5: The Calculator Catastrophe

So, you've embraced the future by creating a pricing calculator or estimator tool. Bravo! You're ahead of the curve.

But before you pat yourself on the back too vigorously, let's talk about how these powerful tools can go terribly wrong.

I've seen countless businesses implement pricing calculators that end up gathering dust rather than generating leads. Here are the most common mistakes:

- **The hidden gem syndrome**: burying your calculator deep in your website instead of featuring it prominently on your homepage. Your pricing tool deserves prime real estate where visitors can find it within those crucial first 10 seconds.

- **The wimpy call-to-action**: using bland CTAs like "Calculator" or "Estimate" instead of compelling phrases like "Get Instant Estimate" that promise both immediacy and value.

- **The dead-end experience**: failing to include a follow-up CTA after users get their estimate. Always guide them to a next step while their interest is at its peak—whether that's scheduling a consultation or refining their quote.

- **The missing qualification questions**: focusing only on price inputs while ignoring crucial qualifiers such as purchase timeframe, communication preferences, or budget constraints—information that helps you understand the lead's quality.

- **The premature information gate**: asking for contact details upfront rather than at the end of the process. Let users see the value they're getting before you ask for their information.

- **The lead quality confusion**: getting frustrated with a broader variety of leads without having a proper nurturing strategy in place. Not every calculator user will be ready to buy immediately—develop remarketing and nurturing systems to guide them through their buying journey.

When implemented correctly, pricing calculators can be your website's hardest-working sales tools.

They pre-qualify leads, educate customers, and collect valuable data—all while you sleep.

But they require thoughtful design and continuous refinement to avoid becoming digital paperweights.

Price Talk Pays Off

Let's wrap this up with a few key points to remember:

1. For 90% of businesses, the number one trafficked search has to do with money. People want to know about the price. It's not just important—it's crucial.

2. Is it possible to talk a lot more about price on your website? The answer is a resounding yes. Not only is it possible, but it's also necessary for today's information-driven consumer.

3. Why do we need to educate potential customers about pricing? Simple: to earn their trust. If we don't earn it, they'll give it to someone else—probably a competitor who's more open about their pricing.

4. Do you need to put a full price list on your website? That's your call. Many businesses choose to put their "floor" or starting prices. The

key is to provide enough information for potential customers to understand if you're in their ballpark.

Remember, talking about price on your website isn't just about numbers. **It's about building trust, qualifying leads, and positioning yourself as a transparent, customer-focused business.**

It's about respecting your potential customers' time and intelligence. And ultimately, it's about setting yourself apart in a market where too many businesses are still playing hide-and-seek with their pricing.

So, are you ready to break the price tag taboo?

Chapter Summary

- Focus 80% of pricing content on industry/market context and only 20% on your specific pricing to provide valuable education.

- Make pricing information easily accessible through clear website navigation—customers will leave if they can't find it within 10 seconds.

- Avoid vague phrases like "competitive pricing"—provide meaningful information through ranges, tiers or calculators even if exact quotes aren't possible.

- Use clear language and avoid industry jargon—explain terms, provide context, and use visuals to help customers understand value.

- When using pricing calculators, ensure they're prominently displayed with strong CTAs, appropriate qualification questions, and proper lead nurturing strategies.

CHAPTER 21

BLUEPRINT Step 4: Engagement - Building Meaningful Connections

"Subscribe to our newsletter!"

Delete.

If that's your idea of engagement, we need to have a serious talk. **Real engagement isn't about collecting email addresses; it's about creating genuine connections.**

In the previous chapters, we explored how to understand your audience, educate them effectively, and build trust through transparency. Now it's time to turn that foundation into meaningful engagement.

Your potential customer has just found your content. They're interested. They're learning. But now comes the crucial moment: do they hit subscribe, or do they bounce? The difference often lies not in what you're offering, but in how you're offering it.

In the upcoming chapters, we'll explore three critical aspects of engagement. You'll learn how *Grammarly* transformed their lead capture strategy to gain millions of users, why most businesses get social media completely wrong, and how zero-click content is changing the game of digital marketing.

We'll tackle the art of lead capture that doesn't feel sleazy, show you how to build genuine connections on social media (hint: it's not about follower count), and demonstrate why sometimes the best engagement happens before someone even clicks on your website.

Think of it as turning your marketing from a series of transactions into a web of relationships. Because in a world where everyone is fighting for attention, genuine connection wins every time.

CHAPTER 22

From Stranger to Subscriber: How to Capture Leads That Convert

Back in 2012, Grammarly was a small start-up trying to convince people to use their writing assistance tool. Today, they have nearly seven million daily active users.

What changed?

They stopped behaving like pushy salespeople and started acting more like friendly shopkeepers.

When they began focusing on helping people feel more confident in their writing—rather than just fixing grammar mistakes—their user base exploded.

But here's how they did this: instead of requiring users to sign up immediately, Grammarly offered a free browser extension that provided real-time writing suggestions as people typed emails, social media posts, and documents.

This approach was brilliant lead capture in action.

They solved an immediate problem (helping people write better) without asking for anything upfront.

Users experienced the value first, then willingly provided their email addresses to access additional features like tone detection and advanced suggestions.

They captured attention by demonstrating their value rather than promising it and captured leads by making the transition from free user to registered user feel natural and beneficial.

The lesson for lead capture is clear: instead of asking people to trust you with their information based on promises alone, give them a genuine taste of the value you provide. When people experience your helpfulness firsthand, they're far more willing to share their contact details for more of the same.

Getting Forms to Work for Your Business

I've made every mistake possible with lead capture in my own marketing career. I created pop-ups that appeared the moment someone landed on my website. I demanded phone numbers for simple PDF downloads. I even used the phrase "Sign up for our newsletter!" as if that was somehow compelling.

The results were predictable: low conversion rates and frustrated visitors.

Why? Because adding more fields to your contact forms doesn't get you better leads. It just gets you fewer leads.

Think about how you behave at a networking event. You don't immediately ask new people for their home address and phone number. You start with basics—usually just a name and perhaps a way to keep in touch.

Copyblogger discovered this principle when they simplified their sign-up form to request only an email address. Their conversion rate jumped by 400%[8].

Not 40%.

Not 100%.

Four hundred percent!

The moral of the story? Just because you *can* ask for information doesn't mean you *should*.

You might be wondering: "What's the right amount of information to request?" Let's use the story of Goldilocks as our guide:

- **Too little (just an email)**: You might get lots of sign-ups, but they're not necessarily qualified.

- **Too much (full contact details)**: You'll scare away even interested prospects.

- **Just right**: Ask for exactly what you need to start a meaningful conversation—usually email and first name.

What counts as "just right" depends entirely on what you're offering in return, because lead capture is a trade.

Every time you ask someone to fill out a form, you're proposing a trade. You're saying, "If you give me this information, I'll give you something valuable in return."

Most businesses focus entirely on what they want to get, rather than what they're going to give.

Here's what I mean:

- **Bad trade**: "Give me your email address to join our mailing list."

- **Good trade**: "Get our free guide to doubling your website traffic."

- **Great trade**: "Discover the exact blueprint we used to grow our traffic from 0 to 500,000 monthly visitors (complete with templates)."

The first example offers nothing valuable. The second is better but generic. The third is specific, promising, and clearly valuable.

Finding the Sweet Spot: Marketing Automation vs. the Human Touch

Once you've made a fair trade and captured that lead, marketing automation lets you build relationships at scale in a meaningful way. But there's a catch.

Just because you *can* automate everything doesn't mean you *should*. I learned this lesson when I tried to fully automate my email sequence for new subscribers. The open rates looked decent, but response rates were terrible.

Why? I had forgotten the human element.

The real magic happens when you combine automation with personalisation. Sending a welcome email immediately after sign-up can be automated, because it still feels like a personal greeting. Similarly, you might automate emails that provide relevant content based on subscriber behaviour or link clicks.

But automation feels artificial when you send the same generic newsletter to everyone, or when your emails contain obvious technical errors.

I've been on the receiving end of this. Twice in one week, I received emails from my local gym with personalisation tokens that didn't display correctly. One email even had a button that said: "Insert button text here!"

These differences might seem small, but the impact is significant. Companies that take lead nurturing seriously generate, on average, 50% more sales-ready leads at 33% lower cost compared to their competitors[9].

The Three Rules of Lead Capture

After years of testing different lead capture approaches, I've found these three rules to be consistently true:

1. Make it clear what people will get in return for their information.

2. Ask for the minimum information needed to deliver value.

3. Follow up quickly and personally (even if it's automated).

With these rules in mind, here's what you should do right now:

First, look at your main lead capture form. Would you fill it out if you were a visitor? Be honest with yourself.

Second, check your automated follow-up sequence. Does it feel personal or robotic?

Third, review your lead magnet. Is it something people want, or just something you want to give them?

The way you capture leads might seem like a small detail in your marketing strategy, but small habits compound into remarkable results over time.

Think about what happens when you improve your lead capture process:

- More visitors become subscribers

- More subscribers become customers

- More customers become repeat buyers

- More repeat buyers become advocates for your business

Each step in this chain multiplies the effect of the previous one. If you improve your lead capture rate by just 10%, that improvement ripples through your entire business.

But this improvement doesn't happen overnight. Like any good habit, effective lead capture requires consistency. You need to test different approaches, measure the results, and continuously refine your process.

The best lead capture systems aren't built in a day. They're built through small, incremental improvements that compound over time.

Remember that every person who visits your website is a potential relationship, not just a potential lead. Each submission in your lead capture form represents a real person who has decided to trust you with their information.

That trust is both valuable and fragile. **Once broken, it's nearly impossible to rebuild.**

When someone subscribes to your email list, they're not just giving you their email address. They're giving you permission to enter their inbox—a space that's becoming increasingly personal and protected in the digital world.

Treat that permission with respect.

Deliver on your promises.

Provide value before asking for anything in return.

Because the way you start determines how likely you are to continue.

_____ *Chapter Summary* _____

- Effective lead capture requires a fair trade. Offer clear value rather than just asking for contact information.

- Simplify your forms to request only essential details. Copyblogger saw a 400% conversion increase by reducing field requirements.

- Balance automation with personalisation. Welcome emails can be automatic but should still feel human and relevant.

- Follow the three rules: clarify what people receive, ask for minimum information, and follow up quickly and personally.

- Small improvements to your lead capture process compound over time, affecting every stage of your customer journey.

CHAPTER 23

The Social Revolution: Why Most Businesses Get Social Media Wrong

"Just had another productive meeting with the team! #blessed #motivated #entrepreneur"

Crickets.

Meanwhile, a burger chain's witty response to a competitor receives millions of views and transforms their brand perception overnight.

This is modern social media: where real connections beat carefully crafted corporate messages every time.

Most businesses waste their time on social media. I know because I used to be one of them.

Early in my career, I treated every platform the same way, posting identical corporate updates and promotional messages across LinkedIn, Twitter and Facebook.

I scheduled content weeks in advance, making sure each post matched our brand guidelines and marketing goals.

The outcome was predictable: almost no engagement, zero conversations, and a growing feeling that social media "just doesn't work for our industry."

The problem wasn't the platforms. The problem was my approach. I was using social media like a megaphone when it's actually a telephone. I was broadcasting when I should have been having conversations. Selling when I should have been helping. Talking when I should have been listening.

Each Platform Has Its Own Culture

Think of social platforms as different physical spaces. LinkedIn is a business conference. Instagram is an art gallery. Facebook is a community centre. Each has its own unwritten rules and acceptable behaviours.

You wouldn't shout your elevator pitch in an art gallery. You wouldn't start a business meeting with memes. So why do so many businesses use the same approach across every platform?

According to Sprout Social, 57% of consumers spend more with brands they feel connected to on social media[10].

That word is important: **connected**.

Not sold to.

Not marketed to.

Connected.

This connection comes from understanding what makes each platform unique and participating in a way that feels natural within that space.

Knowing What Content Is Right

"But what should we post?"

This question reveals the fundamental problem with how businesses approach social media. They start with what they want to say rather than what their audience wants to hear.

They worry about filling content calendars instead of starting conversations. They focus on how often they post instead of how much value they provide.

Remember when teenager Carter Wilkerson asked Wendy's how many retweets he'd need for a year of free chicken nuggets?

Wendy's didn't respond with a promotional message about their latest deals. They didn't run the response through multiple approval layers. They simply responded with personality: "18 million."

That single response became the most retweeted post at the time and gained Wendy's over 3.5 million followers[11].

This wasn't luck. Wendy's had spent months developing their voice and building relationships. When their moment came, they were ready.

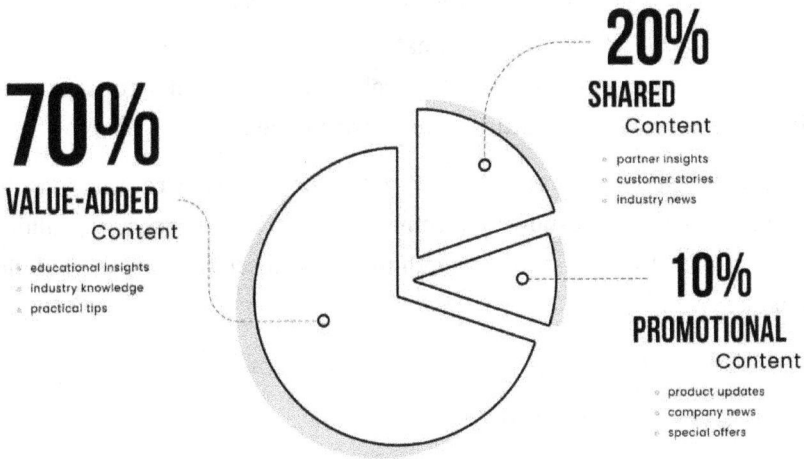

70%
VALUE-ADDED
Content
- educational insights
- industry knowledge
- practical tips

20%
SHARED
Content
- partner insights
- customer stories
- industry news

10%
PROMOTIONAL
Content
- product updates
- company news
- special offers

The 70-20-10 Rule

There are countless articles telling you what to post on each platform. Rather than getting lost in the details, here's a simple framework that works across all platforms:

- **70% value-added content**: This content showcases your expertise. Share educational insights, industry knowledge, and practical tips that help your audience grow.

- **20% shared content**: This is content that doesn't come from you. It might be customer stories, partner insights, or industry news, but always shared with your unique perspective.

- **10% promotional content**: This is where your business takes centre stage. Share product updates, company news, and special offers, but position them as solutions to problems.

This ratio ensures you're giving far more than you're asking—a basic principle of building relationships. But if you're still not convinced, let's look at an example: JetBlue.

JetBlue handles flight delays on Twitter (now X) differently from most airlines. Instead of sending automated apologies, they take ownership, provide real-time updates, and solve problems publicly. They turn potential PR problems into opportunities to demonstrate their values.

Their responses aren't just damage control. They're relationship-building moments that show their commitment to customer service, building trust through transparency—something we've discussed throughout this book.

Taking Stock of Your Social Media

Instead of obsessing over vanity metrics like follower counts, take these steps to reset your social media approach.

First, **audit your current approach**. Review your last month of posts. Count how many were broadcasts versus conversations. Look at engagement patterns and determine if you're on the right platforms for your audience.

Second, **choose your focus**. Select your primary platform based on where your audience spends time. Study its unique culture and define clear success metrics. Commit to 30 days of consistent engagement and document what you learn.

Third, **build genuine connections**. Start meaningful conversations. Share valuable insights that fit the platform. Solve real problems publicly. This is what builds community and keeps you consistently engaged.

Remember that improving your social media approach will involve small, iterative changes. But it's those iterations that lead to significant results over time.

When you shift from broadcasting to conversing, several things happen:

- People start engaging more with your content

- Your audience begins to feel a connection with your brand

- They're more likely to remember you when making purchasing decisions

- They tell others about you, expanding your reach organically

Each of these effects compounds, creating a snowball of positive results. The key is consistency, because the benefits of good social media practices come from doing them regularly over time.

Social Media Is "Social" Media

We forget that **social media was never meant to be a marketing channel**. It was designed for people to connect with other people. The businesses that succeed on these platforms remember that and bring in a human element to what they publish.

They respond quickly, speak naturally, and treat their audience like people rather than potential sales. They make mistakes sometimes, and when they do, they own them honestly.

Think about how you use social media personally. You probably ignore most brand content but stop scrolling when something makes you laugh, teaches you something valuable, or feels authentically human.

Be the brand that makes people stop scrolling.

Remember, social media isn't about collecting followers. **It's about building relationships**. And like all relationships, it requires time, attention, and genuine care.

Stop treating social media like a billboard. Start treating it like a conversation. Your audience isn't there to be sold to. They're there to connect, learn, and engage.

After all, people don't log into their social media accounts hoping to see your latest promotional campaign. They're looking for connection, entertainment, and value.

The question is: are you ready to have a real conversation?

_____ *Chapter Summary* _____

- Social media works best as a conversation tool rather than a broadcasting platform. Successful brands connect rather than simply sell.

- Each platform has its unique culture. Approach LinkedIn like a business conference, Instagram like an art gallery, and Facebook like a community centre.

- Follow the 70-20-10 rule: 70% value-added content, 20% shared content with your perspective, and only 10% promotional material.

- Focus on meaningful metrics like engagement quality and sentiment impact rather than vanity metrics like follower counts.

- Be authentically human in your approach. People ignore brand content but stop scrolling for content that makes them laugh, teaches them something, or feels genuine.

CHAPTER 24

Zero-Click Content: The Art of Instant Value

Search "how to tie a tie" on Google and you'll get step-by-step instructions with illustrations right at the top of the page.

No clicks required.

No website visits needed.

This is the era of zero-click content, where value comes before traffic.

Here's a truth that might make you uncomfortable: more than half of all Google searches now end without a click to any website[12]. That number continues to grow as more people find what they need directly in search results.

For most businesses, this sounds like terrible news. We've spent years being told how important SEO is, spending thousands with agencies, optimising for clicks, measuring traffic, and treating website visitors as our biggest asset.

But think about this: which carries more authority—being one of ten blue links on a search page, or being the single answer Google chooses to feature at the top?

And it's not just Google. AI search engines from companies like Perplexity and ChatGPT have accelerated this shift away from traditional search engines.

Building your house on Google alone is no longer a viable strategy. We must embrace the future of zero-click content.

The good news? Zero-click content aligns perfectly with building a trusted brand. It's not about giving everything away. It's about providing enough value to establish trust while still giving people a reason to learn more.

The Three Types of Zero-Click Content

As of 2025, zero-click content is still relatively new. But I've identified three core types that dominate the search landscape:

- **Answer content**: Featured snippets, knowledge panels, and quick answers that directly address user questions. These are your first line of defence in establishing authority.

- **Rich results**: Enhanced search listings that include everything from recipe cards to event information. These provide immediate value while standing out from traditional search results.

- **Platform-native content**: Social media carousels, email previews, and push notifications that deliver value without requiring additional engagement. This content meets users where they are, providing instant value without friction.

A great example of this in action is Mayo Clinic and their approach to health information.

Search for any medical condition, and you'll likely see their content in Google's Knowledge Graph. But Mayo Clinic is focused less on website visits and more on establishing authority wherever their audience needs information.

Their approach shows that authority isn't measured in clicks, it's measured in trust. By providing immediate, accurate health information, they've become the go-to source for medical knowledge, regardless of whether people visit their website.

Striking the Right Balance

Success with zero-click content requires finding the right balance between immediate value and deeper engagement. It's like a good conversation at a party. You don't tell someone your life story immediately; you share something interesting enough to make them want to know more.

When answering immediate needs, focus on clarity and usefulness. Your content should solve the immediate problem while hinting at deeper solutions. The goal is to show an understanding that different users have different levels of need.

You establish authority through demonstration, not declaration. Include supporting evidence, maintain consistent branding, and build trust through accuracy. Every piece of zero-click content should reinforce your position as an industry expert.

Ultimately, you're creating curiosity. Your content should naturally lead users to want more information, not because you're being deliberately vague, but because you're opening their eyes to related insights they hadn't considered.

Measuring Success Without Clicks

This question bothers many marketers. The answer lies in expanding our definition of success beyond traditional metrics.

Success lies in monitoring brand visibility and brand authority. The first becomes a key indicator of success, including featured snippet appearances and knowledge panel presence.

The second grows through source attribution, expert recognition, and industry citations. These trust indicators often lead to more valuable long-term relationships than simple page views.

Secondary actions like branded search growth, direct traffic increases, and social mentions provide concrete evidence of your content's impact.

When someone searches specifically for your brand after seeing your zero-click content, that's a powerful sign of trust.

Content Types and Strategies

For how-to content, provide the essential steps clearly while saving advanced techniques for deeper engagement. Visual previews demonstrate value and create a natural progression to more detailed resources.

Information queries require balance. Answer core questions directly, but connect them to related topics in a way that builds curiosity about comprehensive solutions. Your goal is to satisfy the immediate need while highlighting the value of deeper understanding.

Comparison queries present a unique opportunity. Show key differences clearly while suggesting personalised considerations that guide users toward more detailed analysis when relevant.

Adapting to the zero-click world doesn't happen overnight. It requires small, consistent changes that compound over time:

1. Start by optimising one piece of content for featured snippets.

2. Then apply what you learn to your next most popular content piece.

3. Gradually build a library of zero-click friendly content.

Each small improvement increases your chances of being featured at the top of search results and AI search engines. Over time, these small wins build upon each other, creating a significant advantage over competitors who haven't adapted.

The best part is that these changes don't require rebuilding your entire content strategy.

Often, it's just a matter of restructuring what you already have—adding clear headings, creating concise summaries, or organising information in a more accessible format.

Getting Started with Zero-Click Content

Start by auditing your current position in search results. What appears above your organic listings? What featured snippets are your competitors winning? These immediate opportunities can guide your content optimisation efforts.

Focus on structuring your content for featured snippets and rich results. Use this as your opportunity to understand user intent and use that to help you provide the most valuable answer in the most accessible way.

Most importantly, measure success through new metrics. Track visibility growth, monitor brand authority, and document trust indicators. These metrics tell a more complete story than simple click-through rates.

The rise of zero-click content isn't just a temporary trend.

It's part of a fundamental shift in how people find and consume information. While the specific formats may change over time, the underlying principle will remain providing value at the exact moment people need it.

Businesses that adapt to this change aren't just optimising for today's search environment but building habits that will serve them well regardless of how technology evolves.

By focusing on immediate value and trust-building rather than just traffic acquisition, you're creating sustainable advantages that will compound over time.

It's not about giving everything away. **It's about providing value at every touchpoint.**

Sometimes that means getting the click.

Sometimes it means building trust through visibility.

But in every case, it means putting your audience's needs first.

- Over half of Google searches now end without website clicks as users find answers directly in search results and AI search engines.

- Zero-click content comes in three main forms: answer content (featured snippets), rich results (enhanced listings), and platform-native content.

- Success requires balancing immediate value with creating curiosity—solve the immediate problem while hinting at deeper solutions.

- Measure success beyond clicks through brand visibility (featured snippets), authority (citations), and secondary actions like branded search growth.

- Start small by optimising content for featured snippets, using clear headings and concise summaries that address user intent directly.

CHAPTER 25

BLUEPRINT Step 5: Pipeline - Building Your Customer Journey

In the previous chapters, we explored how to understand your audience, educate them effectively, and engage them meaningfully. Now it's time to turn those interactions into a systematic path to purchase.

Your potential customer is on a journey. They start with a problem, looking for answers. They move through awareness to consideration, and finally to decision. But here's the catch—this journey rarely follows the neat, linear path we draw in our marketing plans.

In the upcoming chapters, we'll explore the reality of modern sales funnels. You'll learn how Dropbox grew from 100,000 to 4 million users through a perfectly crafted journey, why traditional sales funnels often fail, and how to create content that guides prospects naturally through each stage of their decision process.

We'll tackle every level of the funnel—from TOFU (Top of Funnel) awareness content that educates and inspires, through MOFU (Middle of Funnel) content that builds consideration, to BOFU (Bottom of Funnel) content that makes decisions easy. We'll also cover the most forgotten stage of the buyer journey: post-purchase.

And we'll show you how to map it all together into a coherent journey that feels natural, not forced, because the best customer journeys don't push people through. They pull them forward.

Let's start making those pipelines!

CHAPTER 26

The Sales Funnel: Why Most Businesses Get It Wrong

Back in 2008, you might have received an email from a friend about a new service called Dropbox.

"Get 500MB of extra storage just for signing up through this link," it promised.

Simple, right?

This straightforward referral programme helped Dropbox grow from 100,000 to 4 million users in just 15 months[13]. The real power wasn't in the offer itself. It was how perfectly it fit into their sales funnel.

Contrast that with when I started my first marketing job. I had no idea what I was doing with sales funnels. I drew the classic diagram everyone learns: wide at the top, narrow at the bottom. Awareness, consideration, decision.

Textbook stuff.

And completely useless.

Why? Because I'd fallen into the same trap that catches most businesses: creating a funnel that looked good in theory but ignored how real people make buying decisions.

The best sales funnels don't feel like funnels at all. **To the customer, they feel like a natural journey of discovery.**

Think about your last Amazon purchase. Did you feel like you were being pushed through a funnel? Probably not.

Yet every step of your journey, from finding the product to seeing "Customers who bought this also bought..." to the one-click checkout, was carefully designed to guide you towards a purchase.

Three Funnel Myths That Hold You Back

Many business owners are under the illusion that more people at the top of the funnel means more sales at the bottom.

This sounds logical, but it's wrong. For example, HubSpot's growth to over 100,000 customers didn't come from reaching massive audiences. It came from attracting the right people. Quality always beats quantity when filling your funnel.

The second myth is that the funnel is a straight line from top to bottom.

False.

People jump between stages all the time. Someone with an urgent need might skip straight from awareness to purchase. The modern buyer's journey looks more like a game of snakes and ladders than a straight slide down.

And finally, the third myth is that the funnel ends at purchase. This might be the most damaging myth.

The most effective funnels transform customers into advocates, creating a self-sustaining cycle. Look at Dropbox's referral programme again; every happy customer became a potential source of new customers.

Because ultimately, people don't buy products.

They buy solutions to their problems.

They buy better versions of themselves.

They buy ways to become who they want to be.

Content That Moves People Forward

According to Salesforce, companies with aligned sales and marketing teams achieve 38% higher win rates[14].

But true alignment is about creating the right content for each funnel stage. **Your content needs to evolve as prospects move through their journey**.

First, there's the top of the funnel. This is the awareness stage, where prospects are seeking information and need context. Here, you want to focus on educational content that helps prospects understand their problems. Blog posts, social media content and videos addressing broad industry challenges work well here.

In the middle of the funnel, they're exploring solutions and weighing options. You want to provide content that helps them evaluate their choices effectively. Case studies, comparison guides and webinars build trust and showcase your expertise.

Next, the bottom of the funnel. They're seeking validation and need confidence. Proof-based content pushes them towards conversion, so offer content that validates the buying decision. Product demos, free trials and customer testimonials overcome final objections and build confidence.

And lastly, we get to post-purchase. This is the stage that businesses often forget about, but it can arguably be the most impactful. Focus on customer success and advocacy. Onboarding materials, training resources and support documentation turn customers into loyal advocates who bring new prospects into your funnel.

Your Next Steps

As we look ahead to the following chapters and explore building your pipeline in more detail, here's what you can do right now:

1. **Map your actual customer journey**: not the idealised version in your marketing plan, but the real-world path your customers take. Talk to recent customers about their buying process. What convinced them to choose you? What almost made them walk away?

2. **Identify your content gaps**: this will be key when we get to Chapter 34. What questions are prospects asking that you're not answering? Where are they getting stuck? What information do they need but can't find?

3. **Set up your tracking metrics**: focus on the ones that matter most for your business. Don't try to measure everything; focus on the indicators that truly reflect progress towards your goals.

The journey your buyers take will always be changing.

Your sales funnel is a living system that guides people from problem to solution, not just some diagram on a page. And like any system, it needs regular maintenance and fine-tuning.

The difference between an average funnel and a great one often isn't dramatic changes but small improvements applied consistently. Each step you optimise might only improve conversion by a tiny percentage, but these gains compound over time.

Chapter Summary

- Effective sales funnels feel like natural journeys rather than forced paths, like Dropbox's referral programme that grew users from 100,000 to 4 million in 15 months.

- Quality trumps quantity in funnel strategy. Focus on attracting the right people rather than maximising numbers at the top of the funnel.

- People don't buy products; they buy solutions to problems and better versions of themselves align your funnel to this psychology.

- Create specific content for each funnel stage: educational material for awareness, comparative guides for interest and proof-based validation for decisions.

- Don't neglect the post-purchase stage. Use it to focus on customer stories and other social proof content.

CHAPTER **27**

Top of The Funnel: Building Brand Awareness

You've probably heard of tofu as a food, but in marketing, TOFU means something else entirely: Top of the Funnel content. This is where your relationship with potential customers begins, before they even know they need you.

Think of this funnel stage like the first chapter of a book. If it doesn't grab the reader's attention, they'll never discover the amazing story that follows. The same principle applies to your marketing.

In 2006, Blendtec was just another blender company fighting for attention. Then their Marketing Director, George Wright, had what seemed like a silly idea: "What if we blend things that shouldn't be blended?"[15]

This simple question birthed the "Will It Blend?" YouTube series. They blended iPhones, golf balls, and yes, even Justin Bieber CDs. The results were spectacular: six million views in just the first week, and over the next two years, their sales jumped by 700%.

But here's what many people miss about this success story: Blendtec wasn't selling blenders in these videos. They were building awareness through entertainment. They understood what top-of-funnel content is truly about.

Let me share a painful lesson from my first marketing job. It was 2016, and Theresa May had just become the UK's Prime Minister. For some reason, I thought writing a blog post about "interesting facts about Theresa May" was a good idea.

Did I mention I was working for an accountancy firm?

The results were exactly what you'd expect: absolutely nothing.

Zero leads.

Zero revenue.

What People Actually Want at the Top of the Funnel

Why such a spectacular failure? Because nobody searching for "Theresa May facts" was looking for accountancy services. I completely misunderstood what people want at the top of the funnel.

At this early stage, people are looking for solutions to their problems. They don't know you yet, and more importantly, they don't know they need you yet.

When buyers enter your orbit, they're aware of their pain point but probably haven't heard of your company. What they want is education, not a sales pitch.

Educational content should form the backbone of your strategy at this stage:

- How-to guides that solve real problems

- Explainer videos that break down complex topics

- Deep dives into industry insights

- Thoughtful analysis of emerging trends

The key is teaching, not selling, just like we talked about earlier in Chapter 14.

You can support this with inspirational content that shows what's possible when their pain point is solved. Success stories and forward-thinking perspectives help your audience imagine a better future where their problem doesn't exist.

Consider how Moz approaches their Whiteboard Friday videos. Each week, they tackle a complex SEO topic in an approachable way. They rarely mention their SEO tools directly. Instead, they establish expertise and build trust.

This approach has made them one of the most respected voices in SEO. And here's the smart part: when someone finally needs SEO tools, who do you think they'll turn to?

American Express takes a similar approach with their OPEN Forum, which attracts over a million visitors monthly. They rarely talk about credit cards. Instead, they focus on providing valuable business advice.

The result? When small business owners need financial services, American Express is already a trusted resource in their minds.

How to Create Effective TOFU Content

Creating top-of-funnel content starts with understanding your audience's challenges. You need to dive deep into:

- Questions they're asking about their industry

- Problems they're trying to solve

- What keeps them up at night

- Topics that confuse them

Once you understand these pain points, focus on creating genuine value. **Your content should make your audience feel smarter, more capable, and better equipped to handle their challenges.**

Not sure where to start? Try this simple exercise: revisit the buyer personas you created earlier and list the top ten questions these people are asking before they know they need you. Then create content that answers these questions without pushing for a sale.

Patience is the Secret Ingredient

Top-of-funnel is about making connections. The sales will come later, but only if you resist the urge to push for them too early.

Focus on nurturing awareness through valuable, engaging content, and trust that the sales will follow naturally. Because just like with plants, you can't nurture leads you haven't attracted in the first place.

The power of good top-of-funnel content compounds over time. Each piece builds on the last, gradually establishing your authority and expanding your reach.

By focusing on helping rather than selling at this stage, you **lay the groundwork for stronger relationships and better conversion rates** later in the funnel.

Give value first, and the returns will follow.

_____ *Chapter Summary* _____

- Top-of-funnel content introduces your brand to people before they know they need you, like Blendtec's "Will It Blend?" videos that boosted sales by 700%.

- Focus on providing educational value rather than sales pitches. Prioritise solving problems over promoting products.

- Create content addressing questions your audience has before they know they need you, such as how-to guides, explainers and industry insights that build trust.

- Patience is essential. Rushing for sales too early undermines trust, just as shouting at seeds won't make them grow faster.

- The impact compounds over time. Consistently helpful content establishes authority and creates stronger relationships that naturally lead to conversions later.

CHAPTER 28

Middle of the Funnel: Where Interest Meets Intent

Think about the last time you shopped for new shoes. You didn't just grab the first pair you saw. First, you browsed different styles. Then you compared prices. You might have tried on a few pairs. Maybe you asked a friend's opinion.

This step-by-step process is exactly what happens in the middle of the marketing funnel, or as I see it, the place where casual interest either grows into serious buying intent or fades away completely.

The middle of the funnel (MOFU) is where the real magic happens, but it's also where many businesses miss the mark.

They rush to close sales when they should be building trust.

They push when they should guide.

They talk about themselves when they should focus on helping their customers.

Three Micro-Stages of the Middle Funnel

The best businesses treat the middle of the funnel as not just one flat stage, but in fact three mini stages that buyers move through.

First comes the investigation stage. This is when people start doing serious homework. They compare features across different products, study pricing details, and start to build their shortlist. During this time, they're looking for clear, complete information that helps them understand not just what you offer, but how you stack up against alternatives.

Next is the validation stage. Here, potential customers look for proof that your product works as promised. They read case studies from businesses like theirs, check out customer reviews, and seek expert opinions. This stage is all about reducing risk—people want to feel confident they won't regret their choice.

Finally, the consideration stage is where hands-on experience becomes important. Potential customers request demos, sign up for free trials, and schedule calls to discuss their specific needs. It's the "try before you buy" phase, where theory meets reality.

Some brands nail their middle-funnel strategy so well that we can learn from them.

Take Shopify. Their approach goes beyond merely explaining how to use their platform. Instead, they created multiple detailed guides about building a successful online store, providing a complete blueprint for starting a dropshipping business.

By the time someone is ready to choose an e-commerce platform, they've already spent hours learning through Shopify's resources. The sale becomes the natural next step in an already established relationship.

Anyone who gets the middle of the funnel right understands that people don't want to be sold to. **Instead, they want to be helped**.

The Content That Moves People Forward

Creating effective middle-funnel content means addressing each stage of the consideration process with the right types of content.

Educational content forms your foundation. This includes deep-dive guides that go beyond surface-level information, video tutorials that show processes in action, original research that provides unique insights, and expert interviews that bring fresh perspectives.

Think back to the "Big 5" content and downloadable resources we talked about in Chapter 14. These are really powerful at this stage!

Comparative content helps people evaluate options honestly. This includes clear feature comparisons that don't just claim you're better but explain differences objectively. That "cost and price" content we talked about earlier in Chapter 19? Put that on display here.

Price guides that explain not just costs but value. Integration information that shows how your solution works with existing tools. Use case analyses that help prospects see themselves succeeding with your product.

Validation content provides the reassurance people need to move forward. Detailed case studies show real results from businesses similar to theirs. Customer stories highlight the human side of implementation. Expert reviews from trusted sources add outside credibility. We'll talk more about the power of case studies later in Chapter 37.

Building Your Middle-Funnel Strategy

The mistake a lot of businesses make at this stage is jumping too quickly into trying to close a deal. Remember, at this stage, most buyers are not ready.

Instead, they want to build confidence in the potential product or service they're going to buy. Because when people feel fully informed and supported, deals often close themselves.

So, at this stage, think about the questions people are asking before becoming customers. Those questions can become the foundation of your content in multiple formats.

Creating middle-funnel content requires patience and understanding. You need to put yourself in your potential customer's shoes, addressing their concerns, questions and hesitations.

Focus on content that helps rather than sells, guides rather than pushes, and empowers rather than manipulates.

- The middle funnel consists of three micro-stages: investigation (comparing features), validation (seeking proof), and consideration (hands-on experience).

- Successful businesses like Shopify focus on helping rather than selling at this stage, providing valuable resources that establish relationships before pushing products.

- Create content that addresses each stage: educational deep dives, honest comparisons of features and pricing, and validation through detailed case studies.

- Many businesses make the mistake of rushing to close sales when they should be building trust and confidence through informative content that addresses potential customers' questions and concerns.

- Most buyers aren't ready to purchase yet. They're building confidence in their decision, so focus on answering their questions rather than rushing to close deals.

CHAPTER 29

Bottom of the Funnel: Where Decisions Are Made

Choice.

That is what's important to buyers at the bottom of the funnel: the power of giving them the choice to move from interested prospect to paying customer, or to walk away entirely.

But the biggest mistake businesses make is assuming that as soon as someone gets in touch, they're ready to buy. That's rarely true.

Your website might have buttons for free trials, demo requests, and quote forms, but most of your visitors aren't ready to make a purchase. They're still figuring things out.

When people finally reach the bottom of the funnel, they've already decided they need a solution like yours. But that doesn't mean they've decided to buy from you.

They're now answering a different question:

"Who am I going to buy from?"

The Three Barriers to Purchase

According to research from Gartner, prospects who find it easy to make purchase decisions are 2.8 times more likely to buy bigger deals with less regret[16].

Yet most businesses make their purchase process needlessly complex. They create a barrier which often falls into one of these three categories:

1. **Uncertainty**: People wonder: "Is this really right for me?" "What if it doesn't work?" "Am I making a mistake?"

2. **Friction**: Complex checkout processes, unclear pricing, and hidden information create roadblocks that kill momentum.

3. **Fear**: People fear commitment, looking foolish, or making the wrong choice. These emotional barriers are often stronger than logical ones.

Even the smallest wording changes can make a huge difference to your conversion rate. For example, "Free Trial" vs. "Create a Free Account."

One implies a future commitment, while "Create a Free Account" feels like a complete action.

Same offer, different wording.

The Content That Closes Deals

Bottom-of-funnel content on its own rarely converts leads into customers. It works best when it builds upon earlier content from the full buyer journey. Together, these pieces create a compelling path to purchase.

But if you've got this far into the book, you're probably wondering what the most effective closing content looks like. Here are three types:

- **Validation content**: This shows proof that your solution works. Think detailed case studies of clients with similar problems, video testimonials from happy customers, clear success metrics, and ROI calculators that quantify the benefits.

- **Clarity content**: Use this to eliminate confusion. Provide transparent pricing details, honest feature comparisons with competitors, step-by-step implementation guides, and thorough FAQs that address common concerns.

- **Confidence content**: Reduce risk for your buyer. Offer money-back guarantees, free trials with no strings attached, live demos with real people (not recordings), and details about your support team.

I remember during my first agency role, looking at different project management platforms, and one stood out above the rest: Basecamp.

More specifically, their pricing page.

They don't just list features. They tell stories or give examples about how those features solve or replace real problems. They also show how many companies signed up in the past week.

This combination of clear value and social proof makes the decision feel safer and more obvious.

Addressing Objections Before They Arise

Most businesses wait for prospects to raise objections. Smart ones address them proactively.

When someone thinks "It's too expensive," be ready with an ROI calculator, cost comparison guide, and customer success stories showing the value.

When they worry "Is it secure?", provide security certificates, technical documentation, and industry compliance information.

For those wondering "Is it difficult to set up?", offer a setup wizard, implementation guide, and integration examples.

Your Bottom-of-the-Funnel Strategy

The bottom of the funnel is not about selling harder but instead removing friction and making it easier to buy. Remember that when taking these next steps:

1. List every step between "interested" and "purchased." Where exactly are people getting stuck?

2. Create specific content that addresses each sticking point with compelling calls to action.

3. Test different approaches to presenting your solution, especially the final conversion elements.

The best sales process feels natural and inevitable. After all, the easiest path to growth isn't finding new prospects.

It's converting the ones you already have.

_____   *Chapter Summary*   _____

- Prospects at the bottom of the funnel are deciding who to buy from, not whether to buy. They've already determined they need a solution like yours.

- Three main barriers prevent purchase: uncertainty ("Is this right for me?"), friction (complex processes), and fear (commitment, looking foolish).

- Even small wording changes can significantly impact conversion. "Create a Free Account" feels less committal than "Free Trial" despite being the same offer.

- Effective closing content comes in three types: validation (case studies), clarity (transparent pricing), and confidence (money-back guarantees).

- Focus on removing friction rather than selling harder. Identify every step between "interested" and "purchased" to address specific sticking points.

CHAPTER 30

Post-Purchase: The Forgotten Stage of Turning Customers into Advocates

Think about the last time you bought something you truly loved. What happened after you made the purchase? Was there a thoughtful welcome email? Did someone check to make sure you were happy? Or were you left to figure things out on your own?

For most businesses, the story ends at the sale. They invest thousands in attracting prospects, guiding them through the funnel, and closing the deal, only to disappear once the money changes hands.

This might be the most expensive mistake in marketing.

This is the forgotten stage of the funnel: post-purchase, where customers either become loyal advocates or regretful buyers.

The numbers tell a powerful story here. According to research by Bain & Company, a 5% increase in customer retention can increase profits by 25% to 95%[17].

Yet most companies spend far more trying to attract new customers than keeping their existing ones happy.

Think about that. **The customers you already have represent your biggest opportunity for growth.**

I've even been on the receiving end of this. I remember the time I first hired an accountant. The first sent me onboarding forms in the post.

Yes, you read that right.

A wad of paper, with tabs indicating where to sign, and a postage envelope for returning them. Talk about the analogue age!

Worse still, I would only hear from them around tax deadline season. Nothing in the months before or after.

A couple of years later, I was shopping around for a new accountant, and the one I went with was the complete opposite.

An online proposal, both delivered and signed electronically. And multiple conversations throughout the year checking on how my business was doing and if they could provide me with further support.

The best analogy I can give is that neglecting this stage is like pouring water into a leaky bucket. You need to constantly find new customers just to replace the ones you are losing.

The Three Stages of Post-Purchase Success

The post-purchase journey breaks down into three distinct phases:

1. **Onboarding**: The critical first few days when customers form lasting impressions about your product and company.

2. **Success**: The ongoing relationship where customers discover value and incorporate your solution into their routine.

3. **Advocacy**: The point where satisfied customers become active promoters who bring new prospects into your funnel.

Let's look at what happens in each phase.

The first few days after purchase are when buyers are most likely to experience buyer's remorse. **This is your chance to reassure them they've made the right choice.**

Airbnb does this brilliantly. After you book a stay, you don't just get a confirmation email. You receive a welcome message from your host, local recommendations, check-in instructions, and even weather updates as your trip approaches.

By the time you arrive, you feel like a welcomed guest rather than a random customer. This careful attention turns what could be an uncertain experience into an anticipated one.

Good onboarding content includes welcome emails that set clear expectations, getting-started guides that remove confusion, video walkthroughs that show exactly what to do, and personal check-ins that build human connection.

Once customers are onboarded, your focus shifts to helping them get real value from your product or service. This is where many businesses drop the ball, because they assume the product will speak for itself.

This could be usage tips that help customers get more value, milestone celebrations that recognise progress, community resources that connect users with each other, and advanced training that helps power users do even more.

Lastly, let's talk about the advocacy stage. **When customers feel successful using your product, they become ready to tell others about it.** But most companies never ask, or they ask in the wrong way.

Powerful advocacy content includes testimonial invitations that make it easy to share experiences, referral programmes that reward word-of-mouth, case study opportunities that highlight customer success stories, and insider programmes that make customers feel special.

Don't Neglect Your Post-Purchase Stage

In many ways, this forgotten part of the funnel is where the real magic happens.

It's where one-time buyers become lifetime customers, where word-of-mouth marketing is born, and where your business can grow without constantly chasing new prospects.

And if you want to make that happen, here's what you can do:

1. Map your complete customer journey from purchase through onboarding to ongoing usage.

2. Identify the biggest drop-off points where customers get stuck or disappear.

3. Create specific content that addresses each friction point in the journey.

Remember, the goal isn't just customer satisfaction, but customer success. There's a big difference.

Satisfaction is passive; success is active.

Satisfied customers might stay; successful customers bring their friends.

After all, your best marketing tool is and always will be your existing customers.

Chapter Summary

- The post-purchase stage is where customers become advocates or regretful buyers, yet most businesses focus on acquisition rather than retention, despite research showing a 5% increase in retention can boost profits by 25–95%.

- Post-purchase breaks into three phases: onboarding (first impressions), success (ongoing value discovery), and advocacy (customers becoming promoters).

- Strong onboarding content includes welcome emails setting expectations, getting-started guides, video walkthroughs, and personal check-ins that mitigate buyer's remorse.

161

- Success content helps customers extract maximum value through usage tips, milestone celebrations, community resources, and advanced training for power users.

- Focus on customer success (active) rather than mere satisfaction (passive). Satisfied customers might stay, but successful customers bring their friends.

CHAPTER **31**

Content Mapping: The Art of Right Content, Right Time

Let me share one of my biggest content marketing failures.

During my first junior agency role, I was helping a client produce three blog posts weekly, as well as managing their social media and sending regular newsletters.

We were certainly busy, but completely ineffective.

Why? We were creating content without a map. We had no clear idea how each piece fit into the buyer's journey.

And, as was the case for my client, this mistake is costly. Businesses that align content to the buyer's journey see 73% higher conversion rates than those that don't[18].

The Three Content Traps

Over the last few chapters, we've talked a lot about the different types of content that are needed throughout the funnel.

It's a lot, I recognise that. And you might be tempted to dive in and publish anything and everything.

Hold that thought, because that's what leads to the three content traps:

- **The quantity trap**: Many businesses create content simply to have content, focusing on volume rather than value, and ignoring what their audience needs.

- **The timing trap**: This happens when you have the right content but deliver it at the wrong time, missing key decision points or sequencing your content poorly.

- **The relevance trap**: This is where generic content is used for specific needs, applying a one-size-fits-all approach instead of tailoring content to distinct buyer personas.

Consider how HubSpot uses their Topic Clusters strategy. Rather than creating random blog posts, they build comprehensive content hubs around core topics.

They take an approach where each piece of content naturally leads to the next, guiding readers through their journey.

Recap each stage of the funnel. Each stage has a central theme or question that the buyer needs answering:

1. **Top-of-the-funnel**: "What is my problem?"

2. **Middle-of-the-funnel**: "What are my options?"

3. **Bottom-of-the-funnel**: "Why should I choose you?"

4. **Post-purchase**: "Have I made the right decision?"

Most businesses get stuck because they don't keep these questions in mind. But the ones that do will use this as the guiding principle when creating new content or auditing the content they already have.

If that's you, then **start with a content inventory**. List everything you've created, map it to funnel stages, identify gaps and overlaps, and rate the effectiveness of each piece.

Then **conduct an audience analysis**. Define your buyer personas, map content to these personas, identify any missing segments, and note engagement patterns.

TOP-OF-THE-FUNNEL
What is my problem?

MIDDLE-OF-THE-FUNNEL
What are my options?

BOTTOM-OF-THE-FUNNEL
Why should I choose you?

POST-PURCHASE
Have I made the right decision?

Finally, **create a journey map**. Plot typical buying paths, note decision points, identify content needs, and plan your content sequence.

The important thing to remember is that you want to be creating the right content for the right moment. The best content becomes useless if it reaches people when they're not ready for it.

Just as a good map helps travellers reach their destination, a solid content map guides your audience toward making the right decision: choosing you.

And like any journey, the path is always smoother when you know exactly where you're heading.

Chapter Summary

- Content without a map leads to ineffective marketing. Businesses that align content to the buyer's journey see 73% higher conversion rates than those that don't.

- Avoid the three content traps: the quantity trap (volume over value), the timing trap (right content, wrong moment), and the relevance trap (generic content for specific needs).

- Each funnel stage addresses a different question: "What is my problem?" (top), "What are my options?" (middle), "Why should I choose you?" (bottom), and "Have I made the right decision?" (post-purchase).

- Start with a content inventory by cataloguing existing materials, mapping them to funnel stages, identifying gaps, and rating effectiveness.

- The best content becomes useless if it reaches people when they're not ready for it. Effective content mapping guides your audience toward choosing you.

CHAPTER 32

BLUEPRINT Step 6: Repurpose - Making Your Content Work Overtime

"We need more content!"

It's the battle cry of marketing teams everywhere. **But what if the answer isn't creating more, but maximising what you already have?**

Think about it: you probably have blog posts, presentations, emails, and sales materials collecting dust right now. Each one is a potential goldmine of content, just waiting to be transformed.

In the previous chapters, we explored how to create compelling content and build trust with your audience. Now it's time to make that content work harder for you. We're going to turn one piece of content into many and look at brands doing exactly that!

Picture your blog post becoming a video series, an infographic, a podcast episode, and a dozen social media updates. Or your customer case study transforming into a webinar and an email sequence. Suddenly, you're everywhere, without working yourself to death.

In the upcoming chapters, we'll explore the process of content repurposing and why the most successful content often comes from reimagining what you already have.

We'll tackle the three myths of content repurposing, show you how to audit your existing content for hidden opportunities, and give you a step-by-step framework for turning one piece of content into many.

Think of it as your content working overtime while you sleep. Because in a world demanding constant content, why create more when you can create better?

CHAPTER **33**

Content Repurposing: One Stone, Many Birds

We've all heard the relentless advice: "Create more content!" "Post every day!" "Be everywhere at once!"

It sounds exhausting, doesn't it? Like you're being asked to juggle flaming torches while balancing on a tightrope.

This experience highlights a common problem.

According to research by Curata, 65% of marketers struggle to produce enough content[19]. **Yet most are sitting on a treasure trove of existing material they are not using effectively**.

The good news is there's a smarter way to approach content creation that doesn't require superhuman abilities or cloning yourself. It lies in the wonderful art of content repurposing.

Let's start by looking at a notable example from *The Diary of a CEO*, by Steven Bartlett. Each podcast episode typically runs for 60 to 90 minutes of in-depth conversation with notable guests. But that single recording session doesn't just become one podcast episode.

The team transforms that single conversation into:

- Full-length video episodes on YouTube

- Audio versions across Spotify, Apple Podcasts, and other platforms

- Short-form vertical clips for TikTok highlighting key moments

- Medium-length segments for YouTube and Instagram

- Quote graphics shared across social platforms

What's even more interesting is how this ripple effect extends beyond Steven's own channels. Guests frequently share their appearance on the show through their own written LinkedIn posts, reflecting on their conversation. They might even post Instagram stories and posts featuring clips and send email newsletters pointing subscribers to the full episode.

Before you know it, that one conversation has spawned dozens of pieces of content, each tailored to specific platforms and audience preferences.

But fundamentally, the core message remains consistent, yet the format adapts to where people will consume it.

That's content repurposing in action. **It's about reimagining your message for different contexts, platforms, and audience segments**.

In other words, it works because you are tailoring your content to the ways in which people consume content differently, based on:

1. Where they are (platform preferences)
2. What they're doing (walking, driving, sitting at a desk)
3. How much time they have (5 minutes vs. 50 minutes)
4. Their learning style (visual, auditory, reading/writing)
5. Their stage in the buying journey

The Content Multiplication Framework

In this chapter, we're going to explore how to audit the content you have so far, with the next chapter giving you tips on how to do this with your own content.

Let me walk you through what I call The Content Multiplication Framework. All that work you've put in so far, based on the previous steps and chapters, will fit into one of these three buckets:

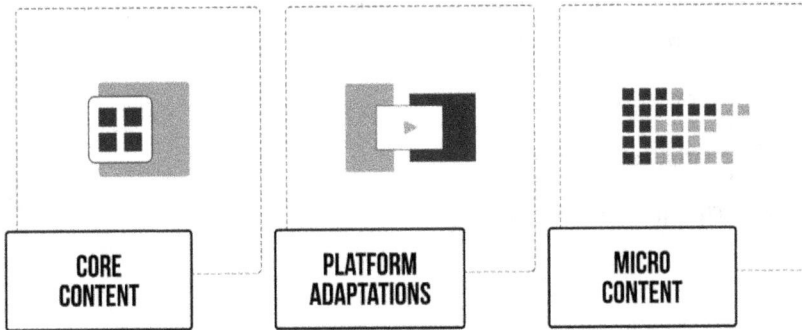

| CORE CONTENT | PLATFORM ADAPTATIONS | MICRO CONTENT |

1. Core Content

This is your foundational material—the in-depth, valuable content that showcases your expertise. Think of it as the stone that creates ripples:

- Long-form guides and reports
- Original research and data
- In-depth interviews or presentations
- Detailed case studies

2. Platform Adaptations

These are formatted specifically for each platform's unique environment:

- Blog posts
- Video content
- Podcast episodes
- Email sequences

3. Micro Content

These are the small, bite-sized pieces that can stand alone but also drive people back to your core content:

- Quote cards

- Statistical highlights

- Tips and quick wins

- Short video clips

In doing this, you'll likely identify some top-performing pieces of content.

Ask yourself: what made them work? At the same time, begin thinking about five new ways you might present the same core message.

The beauty of repurposing is that it allows you to reach people at different stages of the funnel. Someone might not commit to a 60-minute podcast, but they might watch a two-minute clip. If that clip resonates, they're more likely to seek out the full episode.

And the best part? Each piece builds upon and reinforces your core message, rather than diluting it across totally different topics.

Matching Format to Platform

One common mistake is trying to force the same format onto every platform. It's important to remember that each platform has its own native language and expected content types.

Written content should be categorised as blog posts, LinkedIn articles, email newsletters and detailed guides. Visual content is suited to the likes of Instagram posts, YouTube videos and infographics, while audio content is your tried-and-true podcast episodes, interview segments and audio versions of articles.

Perhaps the most powerful benefit of strategic content repurposing is the compounding effect it creates. When you share the same core message in multiple formats across different platforms, you:

1. Reinforce your key ideas through repetition

2. Reach people who prefer different learning styles

3. Create multiple entry points to your brand

4. Build a coherent body of work that establishes authority

This approach turns the content creation treadmill into a flywheel that gains momentum over time. Each piece builds upon the others, creating a network of content that works together rather than existing as isolated fragments.

Small Effort, Big Results

The most beautiful part about content repurposing is the ratio of effort to results. The hardest work only needs to happen once.

That time you put in developing the original insight, doing the research, crafting the core message? Everything that follows requires significantly less effort while still delivering substantial value.

And if you've done that, turn to the next chapter, where we'll explore exactly how to approach repurposing specific types of content for maximum impact.

Because the best content is the content that keeps working for you, again and again.

Chapter Summary

- Content repurposing transforms one piece into many formats—like Steven Bartlett turning a single podcast into YouTube videos, TikTok clips, quote graphics, and more.

- The Content Multiplication Framework organises content into three categories: core content (in-depth material), platform adaptations (format-specific versions), and micro content (bite-sized pieces).

- When repurposing, identify your top-performing content and analyse what made it successful, then consider five new ways to present the same core message for different audience segments.

- Each platform has its own "native language". Tailor content specifically for written (blogs, emails), visual (Instagram, YouTube), and audio (podcasts) formats.

- Content repurposing creates a flywheel effect rather than a treadmill, reinforcing key messages, reaching different learning styles, and building authority with significantly less effort.

CHAPTER 34

Content Transformation: How to Identify and Execute Powerful Repurposing Strategies

Have you ever created a piece of content that took hours to research and craft, only to watch it fade away after a moment in the spotlight?

What if you could make that content work harder for you, reaching more people across different platforms without starting from scratch each time?

In the last chapter, we covered auditing your content. In this chapter, we're going to dive into the practical ways of doing this, and the various approaches.

Because the simple fact is that **most of us are sitting on a goldmine without realising it**. According to Orbit Media, bloggers who update old content are 74% more likely to report strong results. Yet many of us ignore our content archives completely[20].

So, if you haven't done so already, think about the following:

1. Analyse the performance of each piece (views, time on page, shares, lead generation)

2. Map each piece to your sales funnel (awareness, consideration, decision, post-purchase)

3. Identify your content gaps (more on this shortly)

By following the steps above, you will likely find a number of gaps.

Don't worry—this is a good thing and completely normal. In fact, according to the Content Marketing Institute, 63% of B2B marketers use content audits to identify these gaps[21].

But finding them is half the battle. Filling them efficiently is where the real challenge lies. At this point, your gaps will fall into one or more of these categories:

1. **Stage gaps**: Missing content at specific funnel stages (awareness, consideration, decision).

2. **Persona gaps**: Overlooked audience segments or generic messaging.

3. **Format gaps**: Missing content types or underutilised channels.

With this information, you can now move on to the wonderful world of content repurposing, and there are four ways you can do that.

The Four Rs of Content Repurposing

Using this framework allows you to quickly identify the best way to repurpose your existing content. Let's look at each of them in turn:

1. Reformatting

This involves changing the medium while keeping the core message intact.

Remember, each platform has its own language and expectations. For instance, you have written platforms like a blog and LinkedIn, which are great for detailed analysis, comprehensive information and professional insights.

But you also have visual and audio platforms, like YouTube, Instagram and podcast platforms. Reformatting means taking your existing format and repurposing it into another for the right platform. For example:

- Converting a blog post into a video.

- Turning a podcast into a blog post.

- Transforming a presentation into an infographic.

2. Repackaging

This means bundling related content pieces into something new. This is a great approach to use for plugging any gaps in your funnel.

For instance, you might have several blog posts on a particular topic that you could repurpose into an eBook, which could then be used as a top-of-the-funnel guide. Other examples could be:

- Turning a webinar into a course.

- Gathering case studies into a white paper.

- Combining short-form videos into one longer explainer video.

3. Refreshing

This involves updating existing content to keep it relevant. This can be a useful way to fill out your middle-of-the-funnel content. You might have existing content that provides a deep dive into specific topics but needs concrete examples or proof points. Other ways to refresh your content include:

- Updating statistics and research.

- Adding new examples and case studies.

- Expanding underdeveloped sections.

- Improving visuals and design elements.

4. Reimagining

The last method of repurposing involves taking a completely fresh angle on your existing content.

Here, you want to think about adapting content across funnel stages or retooling the content for different personas. You can even convert the content into a different format entirely. When doing this, think about:

- Approaching the topic from a different perspective.

- Tailoring the content for a different audience segment.

- Placing the information in an alternative context.

REFORMATTING
- Converting a blog post into a video
- Turning a podcast into a blog post
- Transforming a presentation into an infographic

REPACKAGING
- Turning a webinar into a course
- Gathering case studies into a whitepaper
- Combining short-form videos into one longer explainer video

- Updating statistics and research
- Adding new examples and case studies
- Expanding underdeveloped sections
- Improving visuals and design elements

REFRESHING

- Approaching the topic from a different perspective
- Tailoring the content for a different audience segment
- Placing the information in an alternative context

REIMAGINING

Your Content Repurposing Action Plan

At this point, it's very easy to get overwhelmed. After all, you've spent the last steps of the Trust BLUEPRINT™ brainstorming and creating content, or you already have lots of content that you don't know what to do with.

Fear not. Here's a practical approach to get started:

1. Choose your top-performing piece of content.
2. List at least five ways to repurpose it using the Four Rs.
3. Identify your three biggest content gaps.
4. Map existing content that could be repurposed to fill these gaps.
5. Create a calendar for systematic repurposing.

For each piece you plan to repurpose, think about what the core message is and what really matters to your buyer.

Once you've done that, you should have a better idea of the potential formats and where it fits in the journey. That will enable you to choose the appropriate platforms and set yourself realistic deadlines for creating the repurposed version.

Don't try to fill all gaps at once.

Instead, **prioritise your content based on revenue potential, resources required, and the expected results**. It's also important to consider whether the content is a strategic fit for your business: does it align with business goals, or provide growth potential?

From Strategy to Action

Remember, effective repurposing isn't about doing less work.

It's about getting more value from the work you're already doing. The goal isn't to have content everywhere, but to have the right content where it matters most.

The beauty of this approach is its efficiency. The hardest work—developing original insights, conducting research, crafting the core message—only needs to happen once. Everything that follows requires significantly less effort while still delivering substantial value.

Think about the maths: if you create one piece of core content each week, adapt it for three different platforms, and extract five pieces of micro-content from each adaptation, suddenly you have 16 pieces of content from a single source. Each piece reinforces your core message rather than diluting it across totally different topics.

Repurposing allows you to refine your message for different contexts, platforms and audience segments. **It's about working smarter, not harder, while building a coherent body of work that establishes your authority.**

Chapter Summary

- Conduct a thorough content audit to identify performance metrics, map each piece to your sales funnel, and discover gaps in your content strategy across stages, personas and formats.

- Apply the Four Rs of content repurposing: Reformatting (changing medium while keeping message), Repackaging (bundling related pieces), Refreshing (updating existing content), and Reimagining (taking fresh angles).

- Choose your top-performing content first, list five ways to repurpose it using the Four Rs, identify your three biggest content gaps, and create a systematic calendar for implementation.

- Focus on efficiency: creating one core content piece weekly, adapting it for three platforms, and extracting five micro-content pieces yields 16 pieces from a single source.

- Prioritise content repurposing based on revenue potential, required resources, strategic fit with business goals, and growth potential rather than trying to fill all gaps at once.

CHAPTER 35

BLUEPRINT Step 7: Impact - The Art of Story-Driven Marketing

"We increased revenue by 300%!"

If you're still leading with metrics instead of meaning, you're missing the entire point of modern marketing. In a world drowning in data, stories are your secret weapon.

In the previous chapters, we explored how to create content, repurpose it effectively, and scale your marketing operations. Now it's time to tackle something more fundamental: how to make your marketing matter to people.

Your potential customer will have seen dozens of case studies. Every one of them will have claimed remarkable results, because everyone promises transformation. But they all sound the same—until they reach yours.

Why? Because you're not just sharing numbers, you're telling stories that resonate. You're not the hero swooping in to save the day; you're the guide helping your clients become heroes in their own journey.

In the coming chapters, we'll expose the five deadly mistakes that kill most case studies and client stories. You'll discover why positioning yourself as the hero creates an instant disconnect with your audience, and how scattered testimonials without context fall flat.

Then we'll dive into Donald Miller's powerful StoryBrand®️ framework, a seven-part system that has helped thousands of businesses clarify their message.

You'll learn how to structure your marketing around the customer's journey: beginning with their wants and problems, positioning your business as the experienced guide, providing a clear plan, calling them to action, and showing the stakes of success and failure.

The beauty of this framework isn't just in its effectiveness. It's in how it aligns with the way human brains naturally process information. When you tap into the biological power of story, your marketing doesn't just inform, it transforms.

Think of it as shifting from megaphone marketing to meaningful conversations. Because in a world of endless statistics and claims, authentic stories cut through the noise.

Ready to turn your marketing from mundane to memorable?

CHAPTER **36**

The Case Study Crisis: Why Most Businesses Get It Wrong

When I published the first version of my website, I made a rookie mistake. I didn't include a *Case Studies* page, opting instead to feature glowing testimonials dotted across different pages on my site as quotes.

No statistics.

No detailed breakdowns of how my company solved complex problems.

There was just one problem: they meant nothing.

Visitors would land on the page, scroll for a few seconds, and bounce. After months of disappointing results, I finally realised that the quotes were self-serving.

My prospective buyers weren't interested in what people had to say, but in the impact I could have on their business and had had on businesses like theirs.

It turns out I had fallen into the same trap that catches most businesses: making ourselves the hero of the story rather than the client.

The Self-Centred Storytelling Epidemic

This mistake is a common one. Browse through most company websites and you'll find case studies that follow the same tired formula:

1. Client had a problem

2. We swooped in with our brilliant solution

3. Look at these amazing results we delivered

The focus is entirely on the company's capabilities, processes, and brilliance. The client becomes a mere backdrop, a convenient prop to highlight the company's expertise.

The problem highlights a fundamental misunderstanding of what makes a compelling case study. Most businesses believe case studies exist to tout their own achievements. **Effective case studies should help potential clients see themselves in the story**.

And this problem is often characterised by five major mistakes that businesses make with case studies, which we'll go through in more detail:

Mistake #1: The Hero Complex

This one is by far the most pervasive.

Companies position themselves as the hero who saves the day, rather than as the guide who helps the client succeed. You see this in wording like "we delivered", "our approach solved", and "our team achieved".

The problem? Your potential clients don't want to hear about another hero. **They want to be the hero themselves**. They're looking for a guide who can help them overcome challenges and achieve their goals.

Mistake #2: The Feature Trap

The second deadly mistake is drowning the story in technical details while missing the human elements that make it relatable.

Think about how people make buying decisions. They want to imagine themselves using the product or service. They picture how it will make their life better.

When a case study focuses exclusively on technical details, it fails to spark this essential imaginative process.

Mistake #3: The Authenticity Gap

The third mistake is creating artificial stories that feel manufactured rather than authentic. This happens when companies:

- Smooth out all the challenges and bumps in the road

- Present unrealistic timelines or results

- Exclude any mention of limitations or drawbacks

- Ignore the client's role in the success

Real success stories include setbacks, learning moments, and genuine collaboration. They acknowledge that meaningful change takes time and effort from both parties.

When these elements are missing, readers can sense the inauthenticity, even if they can't immediately identify why the story feels off.

Mistake #4: Scattered Testimonials

Many businesses fall prey to what I call "Scattered Testimonial Syndrome". Rather than developing full case studies, they, as I did, sprinkle disconnected quotes throughout their website.

These floating testimonials lack context, specificity, and emotional resonance. Without the surrounding story, they feel interchangeable and forgettable.

Potential clients have no way to determine if these experiences are relevant to their situation.

Mistake #5: Numbers-Only

Another common mistake is reducing case studies to a collection of impressive metrics without the human context that gives those numbers meaning.

"Increased conversion rate by 132%."

"Reduced costs by 40%."

"Improved efficiency by 78%."

These statistics might look good in a slide deck, but they fail to tell a compelling story on their own.

Without understanding the human impact of these improvements, such as how they affected people's daily work, reduced stress, created new opportunities, or solved painful problems, the numbers remain abstract and unmemorable.

Moving Forward

Here's the crux: the more you try to make yourself look good, the less effective your case studies become.

This happens because self-focused case studies trigger scepticism. Readers know you're trying to sell them something, so claims about your own excellence feel suspect.

But when you focus on the client's journey and let their success speak for itself, **you build more credibility**.

The good news is that fixing these case study problems doesn't require advanced skills or resources. It mainly requires a shift in perspective, focusing on the client's journey rather than your own capabilities.

In the next chapter, we'll explore a specific framework that can help you structure client stories in a way that avoids these pitfalls and creates genuine connection with potential clients. You'll learn exactly how to position your clients as the heroes of their own stories while establishing your role as the trusted guide who helps them succeed.

For now, take a fresh look at your existing case studies. Ask yourself honestly: who is the hero of these stories?

If the answer is "we are", it's time to rethink your approach.

_____ *Chapter Summary* _____

- Most businesses make themselves the hero of case studies rather than positioning clients as the hero and themselves as the guide who facilitates success.

- Companies often fall into the feature trap by focusing on technical details while missing the human elements that make stories relatable to prospects.

- Effective case studies include authentic challenges and collaboration rather than presenting unrealistically smooth journeys with perfect results.

- Scattered testimonials without context lack emotional resonance and specificity, making them forgettable and ineffective compared to full case studies.

- Numbers-only case studies miss the human impact behind statistics. Without showing how improvements affected people's work, stress levels, or created opportunities, metrics remain abstract.

CHAPTER 37

The StoryBrand® Framework: Making Your Client the Hero

Everyone loves a good story, right?

When we hear a story, our brains release cortisol during moments of tension and oxytocin during moments of connection.

These chemicals create emotional investment. They make us pay attention.

Your brain processes roughly 11 million bits of information every second, but your conscious mind can only handle about 40 bits. To manage this gap, your brain uses story as an efficiency tool—a way to cut through noise and find meaning.

This is why stories are so powerful, which then begs the question: "How can we use stories in marketing?"

That's where the StoryBrand® framework by Donald Miller comes in. It's a seven-part system that's helped thousands of businesses clarify their message by positioning the customer as the hero and the brand as the guide.

The StoryBrand® 7-Part Framework

As we explored in the last chapter, the problem is that most businesses don't tell stories—or at least, not good ones.

They ramble about their history, their values, their processes, while customers drift away, looking for someone who'll make them the hero.

The StoryBrand® framework flips this, following the same structure that's powered blockbuster films and bestselling novels for centuries, but applies it to your marketing.

In this chapter, we're going to break down each step and explore why this framework works so well for businesses:

The StoryBrand Framework

1. A Character

Every story starts with a hero who wants something. In the StoryBrand® framework, your customer is always the hero—not your brand.

This is crucial, and this shift may feel unnatural at first. That's OK! We want to talk about ourselves, our expertise, and our unique approach.

But customers care about themselves first. They're the heroes of their own stories, searching for someone to help them solve a problem.

So, at this stage, the key question to ask yourself is: "What does our customer want as it relates to our business?"

2. With a Problem

Heroes need problems to solve, or there's no story. As Miller puts it, "Companies tend to sell solutions to external problems, but people buy solutions to internal problems."

Problems exist on three levels:

- **External problems** are practical, tangible issues, such as a leaky roof, inadequate savings, or poor website traffic.

- **Internal problems** are the feelings caused by external problems, like frustration, insecurity, or overwhelm.

- **Philosophical problems** involve questions of "why," such as why something shouldn't be this way, or why this matters in the larger scheme of things.

For example, an accounting firm might initially focus only on the external problem: "We'll prepare your tax returns."

But after using StoryBrand®, the messaging can be changed to address all three levels:

- "Never worry about tax deadlines again." (external)

- "End the stress of wondering if you're leaving money on the table." (internal)

- "Because you deserve financial peace of mind." (philosophical)

At this stage, think about the external problems your customer faces. How does that make them feel? Why is that unfair?

3. Meets a Guide

This is where your brand enters the story—not as the hero, but as the guide.

Miller points out that in stories, heroes don't solve their own problems. Luke Skywalker needed Obi-Wan Kenobi. Katniss Everdeen needed Haymitch. Heroes need guides who have "been there, done that."

Effective guides demonstrate two qualities:

- **Empathy**: They understand the hero's struggles and feelings.

- **Authority**: They have the competence to help the hero win.

This is messaging I've incorporated into my own website.

Rather than positioning myself as "the expert with all the answers," I've focused my messaging around being "the experienced guide who's walked this path before and can help you navigate it too."

Think about how you can demonstrate both empathy for your customer's struggle and authority to help them overcome it.

4. Who Gives Them a Plan

Heroes feel lost without a clear plan. They need a path forward.

Your plan breaks down the steps customers need to take to solve their problem. It removes confusion and builds confidence that working with you will be easy.

Plans can be simple. Miller often recommends just three or four steps. You want to explain and lay out the steps to make it easy for customers to work with you.

5. And Calls Them to Action

Heroes don't take action on their own. They need someone to challenge them, to push them out of their comfort zone.

In your marketing, this means explicit calls to action. Not vague suggestions like "Contact us" or "Learn more," but clear directives that move customers closer to solving their problems.

The most effective calls to action:

- Use action verbs ("Schedule," "Download," "Start")

- Create a sense of urgency or value

- Remove risk ("Free consultation," "Money-back guarantee")

Ask yourself what you want the direct call to action to be, and whether it will move customers closer to solving their problem.

6. That Results in Success

Heroes need to envision success—what their life will look like after they've overcome their challenge.

This isn't about listing features or even benefits. It's about **painting a picture of transformation**. How will your customer's life improve? What will they gain? What will they avoid?

Use this stage to describe what success looks like for your customer after working with you.

7. Or Failure

What happens if the hero doesn't accept the call to action? What will they miss? What pain will continue? What negative outcomes might your customers experience if they don't act?

This element requires care. You don't want to manipulate customers with fear, but you do need to honestly address what's at stake.

Why the Framework Works

StoryBrand® isn't just another marketing technique. It's effective because it taps into how human brains are wired.

First, it creates **clarity**. As Miller frequently says, "If you confuse, you lose." When customers can immediately understand what you offer and why it matters, they're more likely to engage.

Second, it focuses on **transformation** rather than information. Most businesses overwhelm customers with features and specifications. StoryBrand concentrates on how the customer will change.

Third, it creates **connection**. By acknowledging your customer's problems and positioning yourself as their guide, you build trust—the foundation of any business relationship.

Implementing StoryBrand® in Your Business

The beauty of StoryBrand® lies in its flexibility. You can apply it to websites, emails, social media, presentations, and even casual conversations about your business.

Start by creating what Miller calls a "BrandScript"—a document that outlines each of the seven elements for your business. This becomes your messaging guide, ensuring consistency across all platforms.

Once you've completed your BrandScript, follow this implementation path:

1. **Clarify your one-liner**. This is a single sentence that explains what you offer, who it's for, and what problem it solves.

2. **Redesign your website** to follow the StoryBrand framework, with the customer positioned as the hero.

3. **Create a lead generator** that addresses your customer's problem and establishes you as the guide.

4. **Develop an email campaign** that nurtures leads through the story framework.

5. **Train your team** to use consistent messaging that keeps the customer as the hero.

The framework doesn't require fancy technology or massive budgets. It works because it speaks to how human brains process information—through story.

The Power of Making Your Client the Hero

When you position yourself as the guide rather than the hero, something remarkable happens: customers pay more attention to you.

By stepping out of the spotlight and shining it on your customer instead, you don't diminish your importance—you enhance it.

Think about your favourite movies. The guide is often the most interesting character. Yoda, Gandalf, Haymitch—these characters possess wisdom and experience that the hero needs. By positioning your brand as the guide, you claim a powerful role in your customer's story.

More importantly, you give your customer what they truly want: to feel seen, understood, and capable of transformation.

Your brand is not the hero.

Your customer is.

And when you embrace your role as the guide, you'll build the trust that turns strangers into clients—and clients into advocates.

- The StoryBrand® framework positions your customer as the hero and your brand as the guide, aligning with how our brains naturally process information through stories.

- Stories follow a seven-part structure: a character (your customer) with a problem meets a guide (your business) who gives them a plan and calls them to action, resulting in success or failure.

- Effective guides demonstrate both empathy (understanding the hero's struggles) and authority (competence to help them succeed), rather than positioning themselves as the hero.

- Address all three problem levels: external (practical issues), internal (the feelings these cause), and philosophical (why this matters in the larger scheme of things).

- Creating a BrandScript document ensures consistent messaging across all platforms—from your website to emails to conversations—that keeps your customer as the hero.

Reader's Resource: *Ready to implement the StoryBrand framework without the steep learning curve?*

Scan this QR code to try StoryBrand AI, a tool that combines the framework with AI to help you see results faster with expertly crafted content that clarifies your message and drives customer engagement.

CHAPTER 38

BLUEPRINT Step 8: Negatives - The Power of Divisive Marketing

You're probably wondering why we're talking about problems when we should be selling solutions. Isn't marketing supposed to be about putting your best foot forward? About highlighting benefits, not drawbacks?

Well, here's a radical thought: **what if your problems are actually your greatest marketing assets?**

In the previous chapters, we explored how to build trust, create content, and scale your marketing efforts. Now it's time to tackle something counterintuitive: the power of talking about what's wrong with your business.

Remember, your potential customer is drowning in perfect solutions. Every competitor claims to be the best, the fastest, the most innovative. But they know that's impossible. They're looking for something else—they're looking for honesty.

Maybe they've been burned before by a solution that was oversold and under-delivered. Or perhaps they're tired of discovering limitations only after they've signed the contract. This is where radical honesty becomes your secret weapon.

In the upcoming chapters, we'll explore two powerful concepts: the art of disarmament marketing and the power of division. You'll learn why Marcus Sheridan generated £2 million in sales by writing about the problems with his products.

We'll tackle the three fears that keep businesses from being honest, show you how to turn your limitations into advantages, and demonstrate why repelling the wrong customers is just as important as attracting the right ones.

Think of it as spring cleaning for your marketing, clearing out the pretence, the puffery, and the perfect facade to reveal something much more powerful: **authentic truth**.

CHAPTER 39

The Power of Disarmament: Why Talking About Problems Builds Trust

I need to confess something: I used to be terrified of mentioning any drawbacks of services, whether I was writing about my own or my clients.

Every piece of content we created had to paint a perfect picture of what was offered.

No flaws, no limitations, just an endless stream of benefits and advantages.

This approach worked fine until one day, someone called me out and said:

"If you can't be honest about the limitations, how can I trust you with anything else?"

That single question hit me like a ton of bricks.

It forced me to completely rethink my marketing approach.

And there are numbers that back up the need for this rethink.

Research from Edelman shows that 81% of consumers need to trust a brand before they'll buy from them[22].

Yet most businesses still try to maintain a façade of perfection, not realising that **perfection is the enemy of trust**. That need for perfection often boils down to three main fears that prevent honest communication with customers.

First, there's the competition fear. This sounds like: "They'll use it against us," "We'll lose our advantage," or "It shows weakness." People worry that competitors will somehow weaponise their honesty.

Second is what I call the conversion fear: "We'll scare people away," "It will hurt sales," or "Our pipeline will dry up." This fear centres on the idea that honesty about limitations will damage your business results.

The third is the confidence fear, which manifests as concerns like: "It undermines our expertise," "We'll look unprofessional," or "Our reputation will suffer." This fear is about how transparency might affect how you're perceived.

The truth is that these fears are costing you more than transparency ever would. But there's a way to solve that.

Why Problem-Based Content Works

What's the best way to resolve a concern in life? Often, it's to address it before it becomes a problem.

When faced with issues, most people turn to Google. Yet many businesses shy away from discussing potential problems with their products or services.

This reluctance can put you on the back foot when a prospect asks, "Is it true that..." or "What could go wrong if..." or worse, "Your competitor said..."

The solution? Talk about the elephant in the room.

Smart companies don't hide their metaphorical elephants in the corner. They put them front and centre, saying, "Here's our elephant, here's why we acknowledge it; do you have any questions?"

Marcus Sheridan of River Pools and Spas did exactly this. He wrote an article titled *Top 4 Fiberglass Pool Problems and Solutions*. He didn't claim fibreglass pools were the best option for everyone. Instead, he addressed potential issues honestly.

← View All Posts

Top 4 Fiberglass Pool Problems and Solutions

June 26th, 2017
9 min read
By Guest Author

▶ Top 4 Fiberglass Pool Problems and Solutions   ✦ 16:09

This article is written by Jason Hughes, a renowned expert in fiberglass pool installation. With experience from over 2,000 projects, Jason is dedicated to educating both the public and industry professionals. He serves as a Fiberglass Pool Installation Course instructor for Genesis and Pool & Hot Tub Alliance (PHTA).

If you're considering the purchase of an inground fiberglass pool and have done any research on the web, you've probably encountered some discussion of the **problems** associated with fiberglass pools.

As someone who has worked extensively in the fiberglass pool industry, I've encountered various challenges over the years. In this article, I'll discuss four common issues that can arise with fiberglass pools, their potential causes, and how you, as a consumer, might approach them. It's worth noting that these problems, while worth understanding, are generally uncommon and can often be prevented through proper manufacturing and installation practices.

My experience in the field, along with numerous discussions with fiberglass pool installers from different regions, has provided me with a broad perspective on inground fiberglass pools. This includes insights into their advantages, potential drawbacks, and occasional complications that can arise during installation or ownership.

I share this information with you, hoping you'll never end up on one of those online swimming pool forums pleading for help.

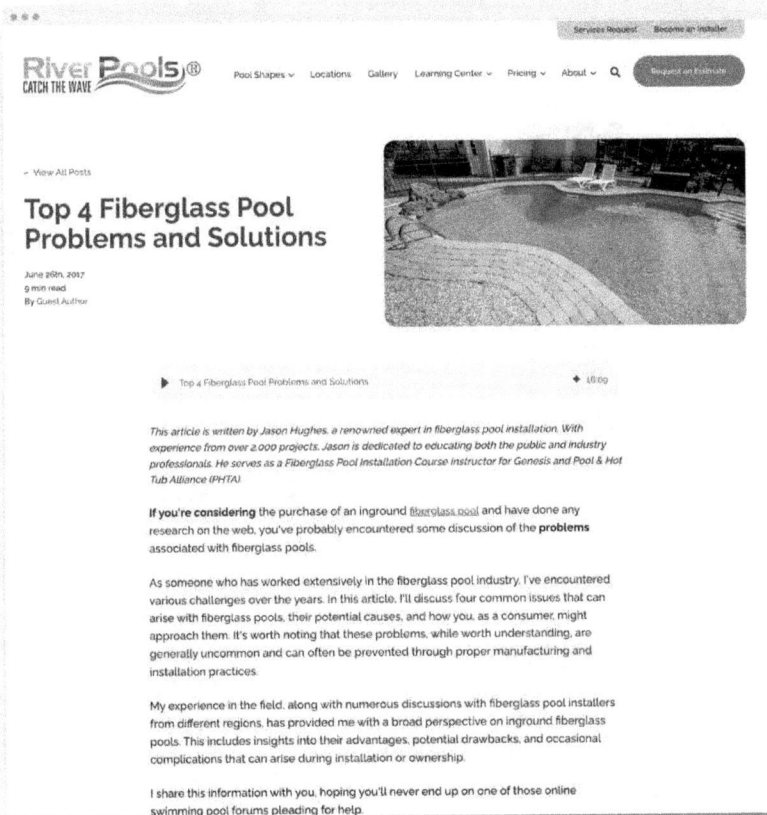

The result? "Fibreglass pool problems" became one of the search phrases that generated many appointments for his company. **This single blog post has been attributed to at least $2 million in revenue**.

Sheffield Metals International, a Mazella Company, followed a similar approach. They published a video on YouTube titled *7 Common Problems of a Metal Roof*. Search "problems with metal roofs" and they are the first to appear.

But that's not all. If you put the same phrase into Google, not only does that video come up, which has generated over 200,000 views in less than two years, but a related video from them also, titled *5 Metal Roofing Myths Busted*, appears in the same result.

And it's not just product-based businesses. The KR Group, Inc., an IT services company, found that their blog post titled *6 Problems with Cisco Umbrella (and Their Solutions)* is the page that gets the second most page views on their entire site.

This is the counterintuitive power of disarmament, where addressing your weaknesses becomes your greatest strength.

How to Address Problems Effectively

So how do you talk about problems in a way that builds trust rather than undermining it? Let me share a few ways to approach this:

For Different Stages of the Buyer's Journey

In the early awareness stage, focus on basic limitations, ideal customer profiles, and general implementation overviews. People need context, not overwhelming details.

During the consideration stage, share more detailed comparisons with alternatives, complete cost breakdowns, and specific time commitments. This is when prospects are weighing options and need deeper information.

By the decision stage, address specific challenges for their situation, detailed support requirements, and risk mitigation strategies. This level of detail shows you've thought through their specific scenario.

For Different Types of Limitations

For product limitations, be specific about scenarios where you're not the best fit. Talk about technical constraints, resource requirements, learning curves, and scalability limitations. Don't pretend your solution is perfect for everyone, because simply put, it isn't.

When discussing industry challenges, address common frustrations, implementation difficulties, market realities, and technology limitations. Showing you understand the broader landscape demonstrates expertise more than pretending problems don't exist.

With cost considerations, be upfront about initial investment requirements, hidden expenses, long-term commitments, and training expenses. People respect you when you respect their money and time.

Time and effort requirements matter too. Be honest about implementation timelines, learning curves, team involvement, and ongoing management demands. Nothing destroys trust faster than unexpected time commitments.

A Four-Step Framework for Each Problem

For each problem you discuss, follow this simple framework:

First, **acknowledge the issue clearly and directly**. Show understanding of its impact, validate concerns, and demonstrate genuine empathy. This step is where many businesses fail, because they try to minimise problems instead of acknowledging them honestly.

Next, **provide context around why the issue exists**. Explain industry norms, technical limitations, and how your situation compares to alternatives. This helps people understand the "why" behind the challenge.

Then, **address the problem by presenting current solutions**, sharing effective workarounds, and outlining support systems. Show that while the problem exists, you're not ignoring it.

Finally, **reframe the conversation with a broader perspective**. Highlight alternative benefits, learning opportunities, and share success stories of others who've overcome similar challenges.

The Results of Honest Communication

What happens when you embrace this level of transparency? The benefits might surprise you.

Lead quality improves dramatically. You get better qualified prospects, shorter sales cycles, higher close rates, and fewer cancellations. People know exactly what they're getting into.

Customer satisfaction rises. With aligned expectations from the start, onboarding happens more smoothly, with fewer surprises and setbacks. This leads to longer retention rates and stronger relationships.

In the end, **brand trust grows**. You gain increased credibility in the market, more natural referrals, and greater forgiveness when things occasionally go wrong, because they will. Your market position improves rather than suffers.

Put this approach into practice by creating specific types of content:

Develop problem-focused pieces like *Is [Product] Right for You?* or *Common Challenges with [Solution]* that address limitations head-on.

Create honest comparison content such as *Us vs. Them: An Honest Comparison* or *When to Choose Something Else* that helps prospects make truly informed decisions.

Share educational content about implementation stories, hidden costs, and both success and failure scenarios. This teaches while building trust.

Your Action Plan

Here's how to start applying these principles today:

1. List your product's top three limitations or challenges. Be brutally honest.

2. Create content that addresses each one openly and constructively.

3. Share these pieces with your sales team and gather their feedback.

4. Monitor the impact on your lead quality and sales conversations.

Remember, transparency isn't about highlighting problems for their own sake but about building trust through honesty.

Let's come full circle to Marcus Sheridan's pool article. It worked because it answered questions prospects were already asking. But more importantly, it worked because it showed respect for the reader's intelligence.

What would happen if you treated your prospects the same way? If you trusted them with the truth about your product or service?

The reality is that no product or service is perfect for everyone. By being honest about who you're not right for, you demonstrate integrity and attract the people you can truly help.

Your honesty won't drive people away. It will attract the right people to you. And in business, connecting with the right people is everything.

Focus on being honest about your limitations. It might feel uncomfortable at first, but that discomfort is the first step towards building deeper trust with your audience.

It starts with a simple question: What truth about your business have you been afraid to share?

_____ *Chapter Summary* _____

- Being transparent about product limitations builds trust, as shown by Marcus Sheridan's fibreglass pools article that generated £2 million in sales by discussing drawbacks.

- Most businesses avoid transparency due to three fears: competition fear ("they'll use it against us"), conversion fear ("we'll scare people away"), and confidence fear ("we'll look unprofessional").

- Address limitations effectively by following a four-step framework: acknowledge the issue directly, provide context about why it exists, present current solutions, and reframe with a broader perspective.

- Transparency improves lead quality (better qualified prospects, shorter sales cycles), increases customer satisfaction (aligned expectations), and strengthens brand trust (greater credibility and forgiveness).

- Create problem-focused content like *Is [Product] Right for You?*, honest comparison pieces, and implementation stories that respect your audience's intelligence rather than pretending your solution is perfect for everyone.

CHAPTER 40

Good Marketing Divides: The Power of Saying "Not for You"

"But won't that turn people away?"

Yes. That's exactly the point.

When Apple launched their "I'm a Mac" campaign in 2006, they didn't just promote their computers. They deliberately alienated PC users. In their adverts, they portrayed PC users as stuffy, outdated bureaucrats, while Mac users were creative, laid-back innovators.

This seems like marketing madness at first glance. Why would you intentionally push potential customers away?

Yet the campaign ran for four years and helped drive Apple's most successful decade ever, increasing their market share from 3% to 7.4% in the US market alone. The fascinating part? They didn't win by converting PC users. They won by strengthening their connection with people who already shared their values.

The mistake businesses make is trying to please everyone. According to research from Siegel+Gale, brands with strong positioning that deliberately exclude certain segments outperform their "something for everyone" competitors by 47%[23].

The Three Myths About Market Size

There are three dangerous myths about market size that keep companies from focusing their efforts.

First, there's the numbers myth. This sounds like: "A bigger market equals better business" or "We need everyone we can get." This myth assumes that more leads are always better, regardless of quality or fit.

Second is the conversion myth: "We can convince anyone" or "It's just about education." This belief suggests that with enough marketing, anyone can be turned into a customer, ignoring fundamental differences in values and needs.

The third is the growth myth: "Any customer is a good customer" or "Revenue is revenue." This dangerous idea overlooks the hidden costs of serving the wrong customers, from support headaches to reputation damage.

Each of these myths leads businesses down the same path: trying to be everything to everyone and ultimately becoming nothing special to anyone.

Example #1: Patagonia's "Don't Buy This Jacket" Campaign

Consider one of Patagonia's boldest marketing moves: the "Don't Buy This Jacket" campaign.

On Black Friday 2011, they took out a full-page ad in The New York Times actively discouraging people from buying their products unless necessary.

The ad detailed the environmental costs of their best-selling R2 jacket: 135 litres of water wasted and enough emissions to fill 66 cars. They even admitted their own role in the problem: "This jacket comes with an environmental cost higher than its price."

Most marketing experts would call this commercial suicide. Telling people not to buy your product on the biggest shopping day of the year? Madness!

Yet their sales increased by 30% in 2012 and another 6% in 2013. But here's what most people miss: they weren't just being provocative for its own sake. They were deliberately alienating consumers who didn't share their environmental values while strengthening their connection with those who did.

This principle continues today. In 2020, they sewed labels reading "Vote the Assholes Out" into their shorts, referring to politicians who deny climate change. They lost some customers, certainly. But they gained more loyal ones.

Example #2: Nike's "Believe in Something" Campaign

When Nike featured Colin Kaepernick in their 2018 "Believe in Something" campaign, they knew it would spark controversy. Kaepernick, who had knelt during the national anthem to protest racial injustice, was a divisive figure in American culture.

The immediate reaction was predictable:

- #NikeBoycott trended on Twitter
- People burned their Nike shoes in protest
- The company's stock dropped 3% initially

But Nike understood something deeper: their core audience—young, urban, progressive—aligned more with Kaepernick's values than with his critics. The results spoke for themselves:

- Online sales increased 31% in the days following the campaign
- Stock price rose 6.2% by year's end
- Brand value increased by £6 billion

Nike wasn't trying to win over everyone. They were making a clear statement about their values and who they stood with, and in doing so, they formed a deeper connection with their core customers.

How to Divide Your Audience, Strategically

Dividing your audience is about strategic focus.

You can create divisions based on values, like Patagonia's environmental commitment, Ben & Jerry's social responsibility stance, or Apple's "think different" philosophy. These are fundamental beliefs that attract some people and repel others.

You can also divide based on needs. Basecamp is clear that they're not for enterprise customers. Rolex never apologises for being luxury-only. HubSpot's pricing tiers make it clear who they're for at each level. These companies understand that not all customers have the same requirements.

Cultural division is another approach. Mailchimp's quirky brand voice won't appeal to everyone, and they're fine with that. Tesla focused exclusively on early adopters who would tolerate the limitations of first-generation electric vehicles.

Implementing this approach requires courage but follows a straightforward process.

Start with your content strategy. Here are some ideas:

- Create clear positioning statements like "We're not for everyone, and here's why"

- Share your values unapologetically

- Make direct comparisons with competitors

- Take clear stances on industry issues

- Challenge conventional wisdom by explaining why you're different

- Be authentic enough to admit mistakes publicly

Your channel strategy matters too. Be selective about which platforms you use based on where your ideal customers are. Target your audience carefully, excluding poor-fit demographics. Match your message tone to your ideal customer's style. Build communities with clear boundaries. Establish rules for engagement and consistent protocols for handling criticism.

In practice, this might mean revising your website copy to state, "We're not the cheapest, and we never will be." Or your email marketing might say, "This service isn't for beginners." Or your social media could declare, "If you believe X, we're not for you."

The Power of No

Consider these two marketing messages:

- **Generic**: "We help businesses grow through digital marketing"

- **Divisive**: "We only work with B2B technology companies willing to invest £10,000+ monthly in content marketing. If that's not you, we're not your agency. We don't work with start-ups, e-commerce brands, or companies needing immediate results. Here's why..."

Which one generates better-qualified leads?

The second one might reach fewer people, but those it reaches are far more likely to be a good fit.

The first message is trying to cast a wide net.

The second is fishing with a spear. One catches many small fish you don't want; the other catches exactly what you're looking for.

When you're clear about who you're not for, something remarkable happens: **the right people pay more attention**. They feel like you're speaking directly to them, because you are.

This clarity does more than just save you from bad clients. It attracts people who are predisposed to value what you offer. They come to you pre-sold on your approach, ready to embrace your philosophy and methods.

These customers tend to be more patient, more loyal, and more profitable. They even refer you to similar customers. They defend your brand when others criticise it. They become advocates, not just clients.

Most businesses waste enormous resources trying to convince the wrong people to buy from them. They spend money acquiring customers who will never be satisfied, who drain support resources, who demand discounts, and who leave negative reviews.

What if you redirected all that energy toward serving the right people better?

Focus on being crystal clear about who you're not for. The best marketing doesn't just attract the right people; it repels the wrong ones.

And that's not a bug.

That's the whole point.

Chapter Summary

- Successful brands deliberately exclude certain segments. Apple's "I'm a Mac" campaign helped increase market share from 3% to 7.4% by strengthening connections with existing values rather than trying to please everyone.

- Companies that take clear positions outperform "something for everyone" competitors by 47%, as seen with Patagonia's "Don't Buy This Jacket" campaign that increased sales by 30%.

- Strategic division can be based on values (Patagonia's environmental commitment), needs (Basecamp avoiding enterprise customers), or culture (Mailchimp's quirky brand voice).

- Clear positioning statements like "We're not the cheapest and never will be" or "If you believe X, we're not for you" attract better-qualified leads who are predisposed to value what you offer.

- The right customers require less convincing, stay longer, refer you to similar clients, and become brand advocates, making it more profitable to focus on serving them well rather than trying to attract everyone.

CHAPTER **41**

Guest Chapter - What is Repelling Content?

When I speak to people about repelling content, they become excited. Not because they have never heard of it before, and not solely because it can increase leads and sales.

The excitement stems from the realisation that repelling content directly solves an all-too-common problem: dealing with difficult, demanding clients.

Many business owners have experienced the drain on resources, time, and even mental health that comes with attracting the wrong kind of client. In fact, when we surveyed over 500 business owners, **80% admitted to losing sleep over challenging clients, while 74% noted that some clients had impacted their mental well-being.**

Attracting the wrong clients can drain your time and finances and sap your energy and passion for the work. Even if you're not dealing with these clients directly, they can quickly take their toll on your team—which means higher staff turnover and lower morale.

Ultimately, attracting the wrong kinds of clients can be hugely damaging to your business, and that's where repelling content can help.

Understanding Repelling Content

At first glance, the words *"repel"* and *"content"* might seem out of place when discussing content marketing. Traditionally, content is viewed as a tool to ultimately generate leads and sales. The focus is naturally on attracting potential customers to your business.

However, repelling content turns this idea on its head. **Instead of trying to attract everyone, repelling content is designed to discourage those who are not the right fit from engaging further.**

Repelling content is an honest and direct form of communication. It tells potential customers who may not benefit from your service that you are not the right partner for them.

This approach is not about turning away business for the sake of it; it is about protecting your team's time and energy, and ultimately making sure you deliver a better service to your ideal clients.

Why Repelling Content Matters

There are many reasons why a potential client might not be the right fit for your business. Some may not have the necessary budget, while others might lack the foundational elements required to succeed with your service.

There are also cases where a client might be seeking something you do not offer. In service industries, even a simple personality clash can make the relationship unsustainable.

By clearly defining who is not the right fit, repelling content helps pre-qualify prospects before they make contact.

Repelling content offers significant benefits. One major advantage is that it prevents your sales team from spending valuable time on prospects that are unlikely to result in a successful partnership.

For example, if a salesperson spends two hours a week engaging with a prospect who ultimately does not match your criteria, that amounts to 104 hours over the course of a year.

By reducing these interactions, your team can focus on engaging with prospects who are truly aligned with your business values and offerings. This not only increases efficiency but also contributes to a healthier work environment.

Furthermore, repelling content helps maintain your business reputation. When you openly state the types of clients you are not prepared to work with, you build trust and loyalty with those who *are* the right fit.

Ideal clients appreciate honesty and transparency, and this often leads to stronger, more long-lasting business relationships. Even those who are not a good match now may remember your candid approach and return in the future when their circumstances change.

Creating Effective Repelling Content

Creating repelling content may seem counterintuitive, but it is a strategic process that involves understanding your own limitations and the unique needs of your ideal client. Here are three key considerations when developing repelling content:

1. How Do You Want To Be Treated?

Begin by reflecting on the ways you or your team prefer not to be treated by clients. This might include issues such as late payments, a lack of respect for your time and expertise, or a disregard for your established working methods.

In our case, while working as web designers, we grew tired of being treated as mere order-takers—people who were expected to follow instructions without valuing our input.

This led us to create an article titled *10 Reasons We Are Not the Right Fit for You*. The very first point was a clear statement: if you are seeking a 'yes man or woman', then we are not the appropriate partner for you.

2. Who Won't Find Value in Your Service?

It is essential to identify those who will not truly benefit from what you offer.

For instance, we discovered that new business owners often struggled to achieve a return on investment from their new website because they had not yet established their brand or target audience.

Consequently, we developed content explaining why new business owners should not invest thousands in a website until they have built a solid foundation.

This type of content does more than dissuade unsuitable prospects—it also educates them and, in time, positions your business as a trusted advisor. Even if they are not ready now, they may return once they are better prepared.

3. What Do You Not Have the Capacity To Do?

Finally, consider the services that you are unable or unwilling to provide. Reflect on the common requests that fall outside your area of expertise or your current service offering.

An excellent example of this approach is a blog post by Denise Cowle, a book editor, titled *8 Reasons You Should Not Hire Me to Edit Your Writing.*

In her post, Denise clearly outlines the types of projects she does not undertake—such as fiction editing or highly technical content—and explains why. She also provides links to recommended professionals in those areas.

This approach not only saves time but also builds credibility by showing that you care about guiding prospects to the best solution for their needs.

The Benefits Of Repelling Content

When you publish repelling content, you don't just turn away unsuitable clients; you actively create a more productive and positive business environment.

By filtering out prospects who are not a good match, your team can concentrate on serving those who value your expertise. The process also ensures that you remain true to your business values and do not compromise on your standards in a bid to secure every potential sale.

Moreover, repelling content fosters a sense of exclusivity and accountability. When your ideal clients see that you are selective about who you work with, they are more likely to trust you. They understand that your services are reserved for those who are truly ready and able to benefit from them.

This not only increases their confidence in your business but also leads to stronger and more mutually beneficial relationships over time.

A Healthier, More Profitable Business

Repelling content is not about being negative or turning away business arbitrarily. It is a deliberate and strategic approach to building a healthier, more efficient, and more profitable business.

By clearly communicating who is not the right fit, you protect your time, protect your team's well-being, and ultimately create a more positive experience for your ideal clients.

- **Lyndsay Cambridge, Co-Author, *Content Fortress***

Chapter Summary

- Repelling content deliberately discourages unsuitable prospects from engaging further, addressing the problem that 80% of surveyed business owners lose sleep over difficult clients.

- Rather than trying to attract everyone, repelling content honestly communicates who isn't a good fit, protecting your team's time and mental well-being.

- Create effective repelling content by identifying how you don't want to be treated, who won't find value in your service, and what you don't have the capacity to do.

- This approach creates a sense of exclusivity, builds trust with ideal clients, and ensures your team focuses on prospects who truly align with your values and offerings.

- Repelling content isn't negative. It's a strategic approach to building a healthier business while creating better experiences for suitable clients.

Reader's Resource: *Want to build a business filled only with dream clients who value your expertise?*

Scan this QR code to get your copy of "Content Fortress" by Lyndsay Cambridge and Martin Huntbach. Learn how to use your website to attract ideal, higher-paying customers while gently repelling those who aren't the right fit.

CHAPTER 42

BLUEPRINT Step 9: Time - Creating Sustainable Marketing Systems

Most businesses approach marketing with short-sighted thinking.

They chase quick wins, burn out from inconsistency, and wonder why their results fall short.

This approach fails because building trust requires the opposite: steady effort over the long term.

In the upcoming chapters, we'll explore how to transform your marketing from sporadic campaigns into sustainable systems. You'll discover why marketing needs a 30-month mindset rather than 30-day sprints, and how my grandfather's carefully preserved 1958 tax tables revealed the true value of timeless content.

We'll examine the TIMELESS Marketing™ framework that builds Trust, Interest, Management and Experience, while exploring the hidden costs of saying, "I don't have time for marketing."

You'll learn how to create a content culture where everyone contributes, breaking down the silos between sales and marketing to accelerate growth.

This last step is about understanding that marketing isn't just another task, but an investment creating assets that deliver value for years. It's about building systems where your marketing compounds in value over time, just like a well-managed investment portfolio.

So, are you ready to stop treating marketing as something you occasionally find time for?

Are you ready to start seeing marketing as the engine that drives sustainable business growth?

After all, the businesses that thrive aren't necessarily those with the best products, but those that show up consistently.

CHAPTER 43

Breaking Down Silos: When Sales and Marketing Finally Talk

"Your leads are rubbish!"

"Your salespeople never follow up!"

If you've ever sat in a meeting with both sales and marketing teams, these accusations probably sound familiar. The battle between sales and marketing departments is as old as business itself, with each side blaming the other when targets are missed and growth stalls.

I've seen this fire fuelled all too often. It's happening in companies everywhere, creating a costly alignment crisis. According to a recent study by Marketo, organisations with strong sales and marketing alignment experience roughly 70% higher conversion rates and over 200% more in revenue[24].

But if we know alignment is so important to our bottom line, why do so many of us struggle to get it right?

Most companies are still operating with sales and marketing in separate worlds, speaking different languages, working towards different goals.

Maybe you've been publishing marketing content but aren't sure why the sales needle isn't moving. Or you're in sales, unsure exactly why your marketing team even creates content in the first place.

But the businesses that break down those barriers see something remarkable happen: they close deals faster, increase revenue faster and grow exponentially faster.

Not through more marketing.

Not through more sales pressure.

Simply through better alignment between teams that had previously worked in isolation.

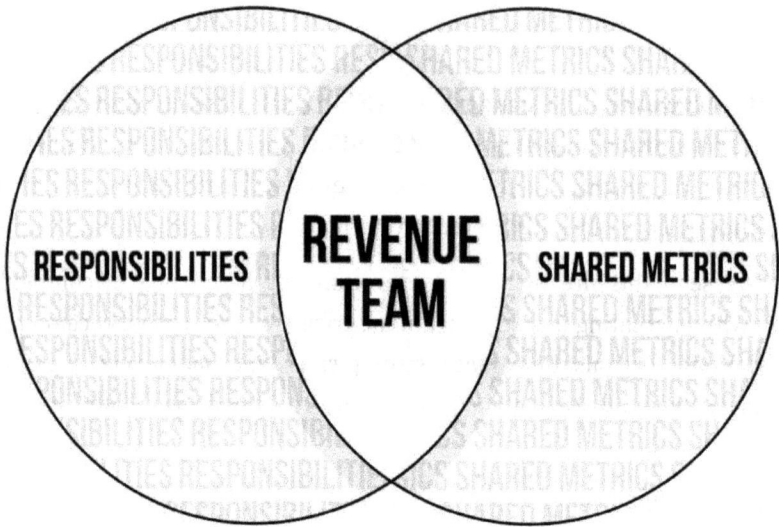

Building Bridges That Last

Creating genuine sales-marketing alignment requires work at three levels: strategic, process and culture.

The strategic level establishes shared purpose and direction. This includes activities such as:

- Creating shared revenue goals so both teams win or lose together

- Conducting joint planning sessions where marketing campaigns and sales strategies are developed in tandem

- Mapping the customer journey collaboratively, establishing common success metrics that both teams are measured against

- Developing integrated campaigns that support both immediate sales needs and long-term marketing goals

The process level creates the machinery that makes alignment work day to day. This involves establishing clear handoff procedures for when marketing leads become sales opportunities.

This stage also sees both teams creating follow-up protocols so leads don't fall through the cracks and building content creation workflows that incorporate sales feedback so both teams can continuously improve.

Lastly, the cultural level fosters the relationships and mindsets that sustain alignment. This means holding regular joint meetings between sales and marketing and conducting cross-team training so each group understands the other's challenges.

Teams should also share celebrations when targets are met, providing mutual recognition for contributions to shared goals.

The Content Connection

To build a true culture of content at your business, your teams need to know what's in it for them—especially your sales team.

They need to understand what, why and how. **The truth is that the right content will make them better salespeople**. They will close more deals, and they will close them faster.

However, salespeople are notoriously resistant to change, so this will take some finesse. Without this understanding, content marketing will feel like just another marketing trend.

Help them see the light. Provide the educational opportunities that help your team learn what's possible.

And if you're wondering what type of content helps sales teams, here are three primary types that stand out:

1. Question-based content that addresses the common questions prospects ask during sales conversations.

2. Story-based content that showcases successful customer journeys like the prospect's situation.

3. Process-based content that explains how your solution works and what implementation looks like.

When marketing creates these types of content with sales input, the entire revenue process becomes more efficient. Sales conversations deepen, objections get addressed proactively, and buyers move through their journey with fewer friction points.

Revenue Team Meetings

When sales and marketing combine forces, you get what's called a "Revenue Team". The clue is in the name—one team united around a shared goal.

That team should aim to meet regularly, but they need the right structure to be productive. **Instead of working in silos, where marketing creates content they think sales needs, they meet with salespeople to discuss which pieces of content the sales team needs**.

Revenue team meetings provide a space for:

- Collaboration

- Information-sharing

- Brainstorming

- Problem-solving

Start with weekly tactical meetings to focus on immediate needs and opportunities. This might include pipeline reviews to track active deals, content needs that the sales team has identified, and other quick wins to implement immediately.

You can then use monthly strategic meetings to take a broader view. Conduct a performance review against key metrics and plan resources for upcoming initiatives.

This is a great opportunity to determine what's working and what isn't, and to make strategy adjustments to respond to market conditions or stay ahead of competitors.

Last and most crucial are quarterly planning sessions. These are the bedrock for setting direction for the coming months. Use this time for goal setting for both teams, campaign planning for major initiatives, and skills development needs. But don't forget to celebrate successes and recognise team achievements.

The Power of Unity: A Tale of Two Approaches

Consider these two scenarios:

In the traditional approach, marketing proudly announces, "We generated 1,000 leads!" But the sales team responds with frustration, "None of them were ready to buy."

In the aligned approach, a unified team reports, "We created content that answered our top 10 sales objections, resulting in 50 qualified opportunities and 15 closed deals."

Which scenario builds a stronger business?

The second approach may generate fewer leads on paper, but it produces tangible revenue results that benefit the entire company. It focuses both teams on what matters—creating relationships with prospects that turn into paying customers.

This kind of alignment is a huge competitive advantage. When your competitors are still bickering across department lines, a unified approach to sales and marketing can help you move faster, respond more effectively to customer needs, and ultimately grow your business more efficiently.

Remember, your customers only see one company.

It's time your sales and marketing teams started seeing it that way too.

_____ *Chapter Summary* _____

- Companies where sales and marketing work together rather than blaming each other close deals faster and grow exponentially, without requiring more marketing or sales pressure.

- Effective alignment requires work at three levels: strategic (shared goals and planning), process (agreed lead scoring and handoffs), and cultural (joint meetings and celebrations).

- The right content helps salespeople close more deals faster, but they need to understand the what, why and how before they'll fully engage.

- When teams collaborate on content creation, they produce materials that both attract prospects and close deals: question-based, story-based, and process-based content.

- Regular Revenue Team meetings drive success through collaboration: weekly tactical meetings for immediate needs, monthly strategic reviews, and quarterly planning sessions.

- Organisations with strong sales-marketing alignment experience 70% higher conversion rates and 200% more revenue than those operating in silos.

CHAPTER 44

TIMELESS Marketing™: The Hidden Cost of "No Time for Marketing"

"I don't have time for marketing."

It's the most common excuse in the business world, right up there with *"the dog ate my homework"* and *"the cheque is in the post."*

I hear this almost daily from business owners and executives who are struggling to grow.

They know marketing matters.

They see competitors building audiences and winning business.

Yet somehow, marketing keeps falling to the bottom of their to-do list.

But here's the truth about time: we all have the same 24 hours in a day. And without fail, we find time for the things that truly matter to us.

When you say you don't have time for marketing, what you're really saying speaks volumes about your relationship with your customers.

The Tax Tables That Changed Everything

Let me tell you a story...

My "fishy grandad" (we called him that because he kept fish in his garden, not because he smelled funny) passed away in 2017 at the age of 90.

His death hit me hard. He was the grandfather who drove me to piano lessons, picked me up from school, and created countless memories that I now see were timeless.

Three months after his passing, as we cleared out his house, I found something strange: tax tables from 1958, preserved in perfect condition.

These weren't just dusty old documents—they were marketing materials that had stood the test of time, valuable enough to be kept for nearly 60 years.

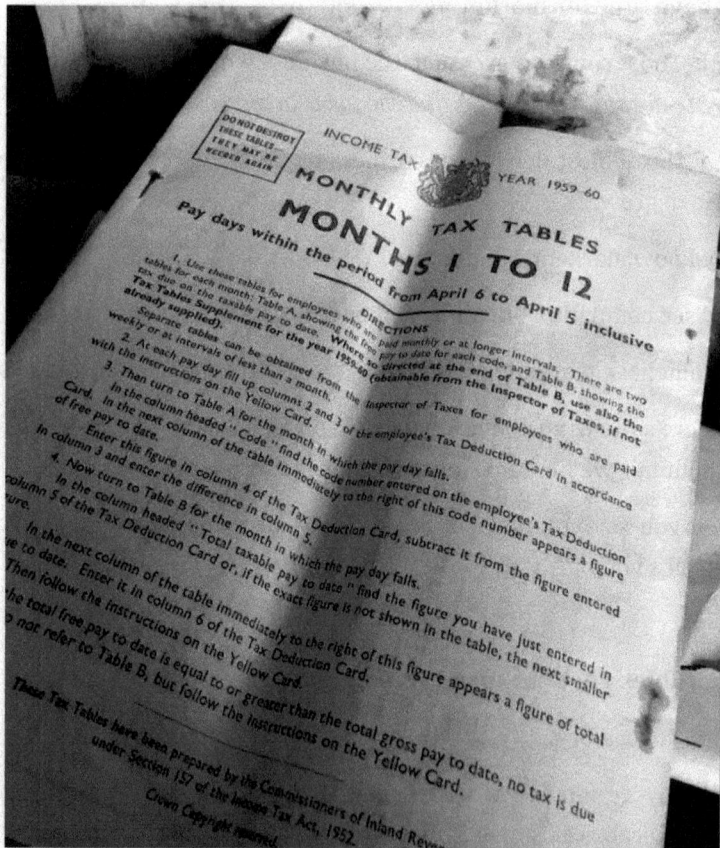

That discovery changed my thinking about marketing forever.

While most people treat marketing as disposable—a social media post that disappears into the feed, an email newsletter that gets deleted, a blog post that gets buried—my grandfather saw the lasting value in well-crafted content.

In that moment, I realised: **true marketing is timeless.**

The TIMELESS Marketing™ Framework: What You Gain and What You Lose

This realisation led me to develop the **TIMELESS Marketing™** framework, and it's a stark reminder of what happens when you invest in marketing—and what you lose when you don't.

Let's break down what happens when you invest time in marketing:

1. Trust: The Foundation of Everything

Marketing builds unshakeable credibility with your audience.

It happens when you create consistent, valuable content that answers real questions, demonstrate expertise through thought leadership, are transparent about prices, processes, and limitations, and show up regularly where your audience needs you.

But trust isn't built overnight.

It requires repeated positive interactions over time. Each blog post that solves a problem, each honest answer to a difficult question, each helpful video that explains a complex topic—these are deposits in your trust bank account.

2. Interest: Beyond Surface-Level Engagement

Real marketing shows genuine commitment to understanding customer needs.

It involves actively listening to feedback and market signals, creating personalised experiences based on customer behaviour, engaging in two-way conversations rather than just broadcasting messages, and demonstrating genuine curiosity about customer challenges.

This kind of interest can't be faked.

It requires consistently paying attention to what your audience cares about and responding accordingly.

It means tracking which topics get engagement, which questions keep coming up, and which problems remain unsolved.

3. Management: The Art of Nurturing Relationships

Effective marketing implements systems to track and nurture customer journeys.

This includes creating workflows that ensure no opportunity falls through the cracks, developing content maps that guide prospects through their buying journey, using data to improve and refine your approach, and building scalable processes that grow with your business.

Management is where intention turns into action. It's not enough to care about your audience—you need systems to ensure that care translates into consistent experiences.

This might mean setting up email sequences that deliver the right content at the right time or creating processes for regular check-ins with existing customers.

4. Experience: Creating Memorable Moments

Great marketing designs customer journeys that delight at every touchpoint.

It exceeds expectations consistently.

It creates content experiences that educate and inspire, builds communities around your brand, and turns customers into advocates.

Experience is what people remember and share with others. It's the cumulative effect of every interaction someone has with your brand.

When you nail the experience, you create customers who don't just buy from you again, but who actively tell others to do the same.

Now, let's look at what happens when you don't make time for marketing.

5. Lost Trust

When you neglect marketing:

- Inconsistent messaging creates confusion
- Sporadic content makes you appear unreliable
- Lack of transparency breeds suspicion
- Competitors fill the void you leave
- Your reputation suffers from neglect

Trust erodes much faster than it builds.

A few missed communications, an outdated website, or unaddressed negative reviews can quickly undo years of careful relationship-building.

6. Eroded Interest

Without regular marketing:

- Relationships become purely transactional

- Engagement drops off

- Competitors capture attention

- Market relevance diminishes

- Innovation stagnates

Interest requires maintenance. When you stop showing interest in your customers, they stop showing interest in you.

The conversation moves on without you, and you find yourself struggling to catch up.

7. Slipped Management

Poor marketing means:

- Opportunities fall through the cracks

- Customer journeys become fragmented

- Data becomes outdated or useless

- Systems break down

- Team alignment suffers

Management failures compound over time. Small issues in how you track and nurture leads eventually become major gaps in your customer experience.

The cost isn't just in lost sales—it's in the wasted effort of having to rebuild these systems from scratch.

8. Subpar Experience

When the first three elements fail:

- Customer satisfaction plummets

- Referrals dry up

- Brand perception suffers

- Customer lifetime value decreases

- Competitive advantage disappears

Experience is the ultimate outcome of your marketing efforts.

When it falls short, the impact reaches far beyond marketing, affecting every aspect of your business.

Trust Is More Important Than Ever

Never forget that today's buyers make 80% of their purchasing decision before they even contact you. That percentage keeps growing every year.

When you "don't have time" for marketing, you're essentially telling these researchers—these careful decision-makers—that you don't have time for them.

Your outdated website and sporadic content send a clear message: *"We're not really interested in earning your trust."*

Think about the last major purchase you made. Did you call a company right away, or did you do your research first?

Did you read reviews, compare options, and check out websites?

Did you look for content that answered your questions and addressed your concerns?

That's exactly what your customers are doing. And if your content isn't there to guide them, someone else's will be.

The businesses that win today aren't necessarily the ones with the best products or the lowest prices. They're the ones that show up consistently, listen actively, and respond thoughtfully.

They're the ones that demonstrate genuine interest in their customers' success.

They're also the ones where **experience isn't just part of the product—it *is* the product**.

It's the culmination of every interaction someone has with your brand. It's the feeling they get when they visit your website, read your content, talk to your team, use your product, or receive support.

The Timeless Truth

Content marketing isn't just another task on your to-do list.

It's an investment in creating assets that will work for your business long after you've created them. Just like my grandfather's carefully preserved tax tables, quality content can provide value for decades.

So the next time you catch yourself saying "I don't have time for marketing," try this instead: "I'm choosing not to invest in building trust with my customers."

Doesn't sound so good when you put it that way, does it?

Your marketing efforts today are creating the foundation for your business's future. Every blog post, every video, every podcast episode is a potential *"tax table"*—a piece of content that could still be generating value years from now.

Consider the most successful businesses in your industry. They didn't become successful by treating marketing as an afterthought.

They made it a priority.

They invested time consistently, even when they were busy with other things.

They understood that marketing isn't just what you do when you have time, but what makes everything else you do more valuable.

The clock is ticking.

Your competitors are creating content, building trust, and developing relationships with your potential customers *right now*.

The question isn't whether you have time for marketing. It's whether you can afford *not* to make time.

Are you ready to make your marketing **TIMELESS**?

The time—no pun intended—to start is now.

Chapter Summary

- Saying "no time for marketing" signals a deeper issue. We all have the same 24 hours but make time for what we truly value in our business relationships.

- The TIMELESS Marketing™ framework shows what you gain through consistent marketing: Trust (through valuable content), Interest (by understanding needs), Management (nurturing relationships), and Experience (memorable moments).

- When marketing is neglected, businesses lose trust (appearing unreliable), interest erodes (relationships become transactional), management slips (opportunities fall through the cracks), and experience suffers.

- Today's buyers complete 80% of their purchasing decision before contacting you. Without quality content to guide them, competitors will fill the void.

- Quality marketing creates lasting assets that work for your business long after creation. Like tax tables preserved for 60 years, good content delivers value for decades.

TIMELESS

Lost Trust
Confusion Through Inconsistency
Sporadic content and lack of transparency breeds suspicion while competitors fill the void you leave.

Eroded Interest
Relationships Become Transactional
Without regular engagement, market relevance diminishes and innovation stagnates.

Slipped Management
Opportunities Fall Through Cracks
Customer journeys become fragmented, data becomes useless, and systems break down.

Subpar Experience
Competitive Advantage Disappears
Customer satisfaction plummets, referrals dry up, and lifetime value decreases across your business.

Trust
Build Unshakeable Credibility
Create consistent, valuable content that answers real questions and demonstrates expertise through transparency.

Interest
Show Genuine Commitment
Listen actively to customer needs and engage in two-way conversations rather than just broadcasting messages.

Management
Implement Nurturing Systems
Track customer journeys with workflows that ensure no opportunity falls through the cracks.

Experience
Design Memorable Journeys
Create touchpoints that delight customers and turn them into advocates who actively promote your brand.

CHAPTER 45

Guest Chapter: The 30-Month Mindset

Let's get to the point: it takes a lot of time to be known in your industry—perhaps 30 months (2.5 years). **Avoid thinking in the short term and get ready to be consistent in the long term**. You can win with focus, consistency, and grit.

When building a business, we'd all love to have a ready-made audience online. The truth is, it takes time—and very few people have the patience to do the work needed.

People often ask me how to get the levels of engagement I do on my LinkedIn posts. My answer is always the same, and it's never a sexy message to deliver: speak to your ideal audience, be known for one thing, stick at it, and then let's chat again in a few years.

It's that last bit that puts people off. They all just want to click "add to basket" and get it done now. Unfortunately, shortcuts here are rare, and this is something that generative AI can't magically take off your hands.

It really does take time to get good at what you do, to be known for it, and, most importantly, to be the trusted person that people remember in their time of need.

There simply is no "easy" button for your marketing. And don't fall for the potential promise of using ads to get yourself seen. That can work for a short-term boost, but the long-term costs of this approach can be high and, crucially, those costs are not fully under your control.

It's far better to invest in building your personal brand and creating content you own that gets you known as the expert in your space. The payoff from that will be far greater in the long run. But even then, your content isn't going to be good from day one.

If you've never baked the cake before but decide to give it a go, your first attempt might be terrible. If you stick at it and focus on the same task every day, the cake you bake in a year's time is all but guaranteed to be delicious.

The delicious version of the cake has an ancestor that's an inedible brick. Before you can produce something good, give yourself the grace to make something bad—that's just the way it goes, in baking and content creation alike.

(If you can't accept the idea of ever producing an inedible cake, you might have some mindset work to do around overcoming perfectionism and imposter syndrome. Those are big topics beyond the scope of what I'm getting at here.)

Let's assume you're willing to accept that everything's not just going to fall into your lap and work out straightaway. The question then becomes: how long does it really take?

Mark Schaefer's book *KNOWN* showed that it can take 30 months (2.5 years) to become known in the right place and space for your industry. I was one of almost 100 case studies included in that book, and by following Mark's teachings I've managed to carve out a successful and sustainable business for myself—and sure enough, it did take me around 30 months of hard effort to start seeing the kind of results I was after.

A common problem in content creation is that people give up too quickly. They commission a new website and write a handful of blog posts, or perhaps they launch a podcast and release a few episodes. That's fine as a starting point, but you must stick at it to have a chance of success.

Take podcasting, for example: the average number of episodes for a podcast is in the single digits. No one's going to get success with such a small content footprint.

Meanwhile, the podcasters I see succeeding are all well past putting out their 300th episode. It takes real commitment to hit a content milestone like that, but the rewards are there for those who make and stick to a long-term publishing plan.

Web search ranking results come from building a significant content footprint on your website, fostering a community who will share that material, and then getting links back to your site from other places on the web. This takes effort and time—and most businesses aren't ready for it.

I blogged inconsistently between 2014 and 2016. It got me little in the way of website traffic and almost nothing in the way of leads for my business. It's only when I discovered content marketing in 2016 that I started to buck up my ideas and understand that combining consistency and congruence was the route to success.

Although I focused on writing as my strong suit, it became clear to me that the need for long-term commitment applied to all formats of content and on all platforms. Whether you're a blogger, podcaster, livestreamer, or anything else, consistency is at the heart of all good things worth achieving.

Whatever your aim, you need to make consistency a habit.

About Grit

Mark Schaefer's analysis in *KNOWN* showed that everyone he interviewed had demonstrated a few key characteristics: focus, consistency, and grit. I found the last of those words interesting, and it led me to the work of writer Angela Duckworth, who, conveniently, has a book of the same name: *Grit*.

Here's a summary of Angela's recommendations. If you can put these into your business, you'll stand a good chance of being around for the long haul:

- **Find love in your work**: Isn't it great to see a small business with excitement and enthusiasm for what they do? We spend much of our waking lives trying to earn a crust. We need to find ways for it to fulfil us.

- **Find capacity to practise**: The best businesses are excellent at execution. You need a way to keep sharpening your blade—not only in the content you create, but also in the core service you deliver. Don't just be good: strive to be great.

- **Find your purpose**: Think about what's driving you at the root. Money alone probably isn't it. Why are you doing any of this stuff anyway? Clarity on your *why* doesn't matter as much to your customers as some people suggest it does, but it should certainly matter to you. Have a reason to leap out of bed in the morning.

- **Don't lose hope**: Business is never plain sailing. Keep afloat. If you've plotted the right course, those choppy waters won't last forever.

    - **John Espirian, Author, *Content DNA***

--------------------- *Chapter Summary* ---------------------

- Building industry recognition takes significant time, around 30 months according to Mark Schaefer's research.

- Success requires consistent content creation and publication. Sporadic efforts yield minimal results.

- There are no shortcuts or "easy buttons". Even paid ads only provide temporary visibility.

- Three key characteristics drive success: focus, consistency and grit (defined as finding purpose and not losing hope).

- Give yourself permission to create imperfect content initially. Quality improves with sustained practice.

Reader's Resource: *Ready to stand out in a crowded marketplace with content that truly reflects your business personality?*

Scan this QR code to get your copy of "Content DNA" by John Espirian. Discover how to define your business's unique "shape" and build a distinctive online presence that gets noticed, remembered, and preferred.

PART 3

From Strategy to Success:
Six Critical Factors for
Marketing That Delivers

CHAPTER 46

The Work Starts Now....
What's Next?

You've made it through the journey.

You've learned the core principles, explored the frameworks, and seen how trust-building marketing can transform your business.

But here comes the hard part: **actually doing it.**

In the coming chapters, we'll explore the six critical success factors that separate businesses that thrive with content marketing from those that simply survive (or worse, give up entirely). **These success factors are the difference between wasted effort and remarkable results**.

First, we'll examine why real marketing transformation requires buy-in at every level of your organisation. You'll discover how companies like Yale Appliance grew from $37 million to $180 million by making content creation a company-wide policy.

Next, we'll explore why even the most enthusiastic team needs a dedicated content conductor. Like Microsoft's "Chief Storyteller", who helped triple their stock price, your content strategy needs someone who wakes up thinking about how to make it sing.

We'll then uncover how to tap into the goldmine of expertise already within your walls. Your subject matter experts have valuable knowledge locked in their heads, and you just need the right system to extract and share it like Drift did with their VP of Sales to generate millions of blog views.

You'll learn why the debate between quality and quantity misses the point entirely, and see how focusing on depth over breadth, and expertise over volume, creates sustainable results even as the content landscape evolves.

We'll show you how content can transform your sales process, dramatically shorten sales cycles and boost close rates. You'll discover how Assignment Selling qualifies prospects and builds trust before they ever speak to your team.

Finally, we'll tackle the measurement framework that proves your content's worth. Just as Moz increased conversion rates by 170% through systematic testing, you'll learn how to connect traffic, engagement, conversion, and revenue metrics into a clear story of business impact.

Remember: these six keys to success—organisational buy-in, dedicated content ownership, leveraging internal experts, balancing quality and quantity, sales team enablement, and systematic measurement—form the foundation of effective content marketing.

By implementing these principles, you're well positioned to build a trusted brand that attracts, engages, and retains your ideal clients.

Remember, **the strategies in this book aren't magic**.

They're proven principles that work when consistently applied.

The question isn't whether they'll work for you, but whether you'll commit to making them work.

So what happens next?

That's entirely up to you.

CHAPTER 47

Success Factor 1: The Critical Role of Organisation-Wide Buy-In

"Marketing isn't my job."

I hear this phrase constantly in businesses striving to become more trusted in their industry. It usually comes from someone in operations, finance, or technical support. And every time I hear it, I know we're about to face an uphill battle.

Because here's the truth: trust-building isn't just marketing's job.

It's everyone's job.

According to Edelman's research, businesses with company-wide trust initiatives see three times higher customer retention rates than those where trust-building is limited to the marketing department[25].

Most businesses have their marketing all wrong. They trap content creation inside the walls of their marketing department, where a handful of overwhelmed writers struggle to be the voice of the entire company.

I know because I've been that person. I wrote every blog post. Every social update. Every case study. And it was killing the marketing momentum.

So, in this chapter, we're going to build on the sales and marketing alignment we discussed earlier and show how you can take marketing from a production of isolation to one where the whole business is bought in and rallied behind.

Why Alignment Matters

When your entire company isn't aligned on your sales and marketing strategy, several problems will quickly emerge:

- **Trust gets fractured**: Customers receive mixed messages that make them hesitant to buy.

- **Sales cycles drag on**: Your sales team spends too much time explaining basics because marketing isn't creating the right trust-building content.

- **Resources get wasted**: Scattered efforts mean you spend more but see fewer results.

Believe me, I've seen it happen. In fact, I've been a victim of it myself.

I remember working in-house and pushing for the senior leadership team to be involved, or even to give me a marketing budget, but I was fighting a losing battle—like pushing water uphill with a fork.

There's a key distinction many miss: **alignment doesn't mean centralisation. It means orchestration.**

Think of it like a music ensemble. If only one person is allowed to play, you get a solo. It might be beautiful, but it's limited. When everyone plays their part, following the same sheet music but contributing their unique instrument, you get a symphony.

Most marketing teams try to play every instrument themselves.

But one voice isn't enough.

In contrast, companies where everyone contributes to trust-building see shorter sales cycles, higher conversion rates, and more effective use of marketing resources.

The most successful businesses don't view marketing as a department.

They see it as a **company-wide responsibility**.

They understand that trust is built through every interaction a customer has with their business, not just through official marketing channels.

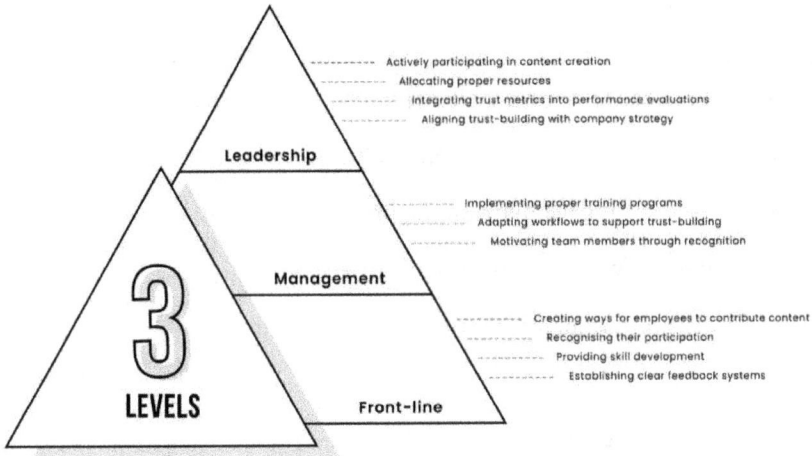

Three Levels of Organisational Buy-In

To create true organisational buy-in, you need to ensure you're taking the fight to three levels:

1. The Leadership Level

True transformation starts at the top. When I work with companies, the first question I ask is: "How involved is your leadership team in marketing activities?"

The answer tells me everything about their chances of success.

Effective leadership buy-in includes:

- Actively participating in content creation

- Allocating proper resources

- Integrating trust metrics into performance evaluations

- Aligning trust-building with company strategy

2. The Management Level

Middle management is where most trust initiatives succeed or fail. They're the bridge between executive vision and front-line execution.

You want to ensure the management leaders are:

- Implementing proper training programmes

- Adapting workflows to support trust-building

- Motivating team members through recognition

3. The Front-Line Level

These are the employees who interact with customers daily and have the deepest understanding of their challenges and needs.

Their participation is vital. I cannot underscore that enough.

Their involvement and buy-in includes:

- Creating simple ways for employees to contribute content

- Recognising their participation

- Providing skill development

- Establishing clear feedback systems

Everyone Has Something to Share

Each department in your company sees your business from a unique angle, giving them special insights to share:

- **Your sales team** knows what objections prospects raise, which deals succeed or fail and why, how you compare to competitors, what questions customers ask most often, and real-world examples of your products in action.

- **Your customer service team** understands common questions, troubleshooting approaches that work, success stories worth celebrating, how to explain features clearly, and problems customers encounter repeatedly.

- **Your technical team** can explain product updates, create technical guides, share integration stories, discuss security considerations, outline best practices, and preview upcoming innovations.

- **Your executive team** brings vision pieces, industry insights, strategy articles, leadership lessons, company updates, and perspectives on future trends.

The Power of Many Voices

Consider these two scenarios:

In scenario one, your marketing team creates four blog posts per month. You get limited perspectives, bottlenecked creation, a marketing-centric view, and restricted reach.

In scenario two, twenty employees create one piece of content each per month. You get diverse perspectives, scalable creation, real-world insights, and exponential reach.

Which builds a stronger foundation for your content marketing?

This isn't just about volume. It's about **authenticity and connection**. When content comes from the people closest to your customers, it resonates in ways that polished marketing pieces often can't.

The Yale Appliance Success Story

Few examples illustrate the power of organisation-wide buy-in better than Yale Appliance.

When CEO Steve Sheinkopf first attempted to implement a content marketing strategy, the results were disappointing. Blog posts went unpublished, videos remained unfilmed, and growth was minimal.

The turning point came when Sheinkopf made content creation a **company-wide policy**.

He didn't just suggest it—he mandated it.

Every department, from sales to service technicians, was required to contribute their expertise to the company's content efforts.

The results?

Yale Appliance grew from a struggling £37 million business to over £180 million in revenue.

They're spending £700,000 less on advertising annually, and their margins are up 5% in what is known to be a brutal industry.

Their website now attracts more than 8 million visitors annually and generates an average of 3,700 leads every month.

They've become the definitive voice in their industry, and customers routinely drive past competitors to buy from them because they trust Yale's expertise.

What made this possible wasn't just a good content strategy—it was getting **every person in the company involved in execution**.

The service technicians who fixed appliances daily had insights that no marketing writer could replicate.

The sales team knew exactly which questions customers asked before purchasing.

The warehouse staff understood delivery challenges better than anyone.

When everyone contributed, the content became **genuinely helpful**, **deeply trustworthy**, and **impossible for competitors to copy**.

Breaking Down the Three Mindsets That Kill Content Culture

There are three mindsets that prevent companies from building thriving content cultures:

1. "Only Marketers Can Create Content"

You tell yourself that subject matter experts are too busy, salespeople can't write, technical teams don't understand marketing, executives won't participate, and customer service should focus only on tickets.

This myth ignores a fundamental truth: everyone in your company has valuable knowledge and experiences worth sharing. They might need guidance on how to express it, but the raw material is there.

2. "Everything Must Be Perfect"

You're convinced you need to approve every word, that consistency means uniformity, that spontaneity is dangerous, that guidelines limit creativity, and that mistakes will damage our brand.

This perfectionism leads to paralysis. When the bar is impossibly high, people stop trying to clear it. The pursuit of flawless content results in no content at all.

3. "More Processes Mean Better Content"

You believe everyone needs formal training, that tools solve everything, that one size fits all, that speed kills quality, and that structure stifles authenticity.

Too much process creates friction, which discourages participation. The best content cultures find the balance between helpful structure and creative freedom.

Alignment Day: Starting with a Company Alignment Workshop

One of the most effective ways to jumpstart organisation-wide buy-in is through a Company Alignment Workshop.

This one-day session brings together key people from sales, marketing, and leadership to create a shared vision for building trust with customers.

The workshop serves as a catalyst for transformation, helping everyone understand their part in building a trusted brand. Teams leave with an action plan that keeps them aligned and moving forward together.

Most importantly, the workshop breaks down the silos that typically exist between departments. It creates a shared language and common goals around trust-building.

When everyone understands how their role contributes to the larger trust-building effort, resistance decreases and participation increases.

From there, businesses that perform best work in 90-day cycles. This ongoing cycle of improvement keeps your trust-building efforts progressing and creates a rhythm of continuous improvement. It ensures your organisation's ability to build trust becomes stronger over time.

Avoiding Common Pitfalls

This chapter might sound like I'm asking a lot. You might even be the marketer reading this saying, "But I'm always asking others in the business for help. What difference will a workshop make?"

To which I respond with the notion that **you can be a preacher to the entire world, but nobody will listen to you in your hometown.**

As I said before, I've been there. I know how hard in-house marketers are working, and the battles they're fighting every single day.

Sometimes outside help can be the right catalyst for change. However, whether you bring someone in or not, there are three pitfalls businesses often face when trying to get more people involved:

- **The mandate trap**: Forcing participation often creates resistance and poor-quality contributions. Instead, focus on voluntary participation, align incentives with individual goals, and celebrate successes. Start with enthusiastic volunteers and let their success inspire others.

- **The quantity trap**: Emphasising volume over quality leads to burnout and diminishing returns. Focus instead on creating genuinely helpful content at a sustainable pace. Provide proper support and recognition and regularly assess what's working.

- **The training trap**: One-time training does not create lasting change. Implement continuous learning opportunities, track progress, and evolve your programme based on feedback and results. Skills need reinforcement to become habits.

__Reader's Resource:__ Ready to get your whole team behind your sales and marketing vision?

Scan the QR code to find out more about the Company Alignment Workshop offered in-person and online.

The Power of True Buy-In

The Yale Appliance story shows us that true transformation requires more than just a good marketing strategy.

It requires organisation-wide commitment.

When every department contributes their expertise to trust-building, the results can be extraordinary.

When Steve Sheinkopf made content a company policy at Yale Appliance, he was not just implementing a marketing tactic. He was creating a culture where trust-building became everyone's responsibility.

That shift in thinking — from marketing as a department to marketing as a company-wide commitment — was what enabled their remarkable growth.

This transformation is not about turning everyone into marketers. It is about enabling everyone to contribute to your business's trust-building efforts in authentic, meaningful ways.

Trust-building does not belong to one department.

It is a culture.

The question, therefore, is whether you're ready to make the commitment at every level to do it right.

Chapter Summary

- Trust-building isn't just marketing's job; it's everyone's job. Companies with organisation-wide trust initiatives see three times higher customer retention rates than those where trust remains isolated within marketing.

- Successful buy-in requires commitment at all three levels: leadership driving strategy, management implementing systems, and front-line staff sharing customer insights.

- Each department brings unique value—sales knows objections, service understands common questions, technical teams explain features, and executives provide vision and strategy.

- The Yale Appliance case study shows the power of transformation, growing from £37 million to £180 million by making content creation a company-wide policy rather than a marketing department responsibility.

- Avoid the three content killers: believing only marketers can create content, demanding perfection, and overcomplicating processes that discourage participation.

CHAPTER 48

Success Factor 2: Hiring a Content Manager to Own Your Content Production

Every band needs a leader. Every film needs a director.

And your content strategy? It needs someone who wakes up each morning thinking about how to make it sing.

You might believe that once your whole team is excited about content marketing, you've cracked it.

But here's the truth: even with enthusiastic colleagues ready to help, you still need someone whose primary job is orchestrating your content strategy.

Without someone coordinating efforts, your strategy quickly becomes a jumble of disconnected pieces rather than a coherent story that builds trust with your audience.

The Content Manager Transformation

This problem isn't unique to small companies. Even tech giants struggle with it.

Back in 2014, Microsoft was fighting an image problem. Despite their incredible technology and brilliant workforce, they were viewed as outdated—the opposite of innovative. To address this, they created a role most people had never heard of before: Chief Storyteller.

Steve Clayton stepped into this position, and many questioned why such a role was needed. After all, Microsoft already had marketing teams, PR departments and content creators. Why did they need a storyteller?

The answer became clear as Clayton transformed Microsoft's narrative. He didn't just create content—he orchestrated how the entire company told its story. From engineers to executives, he helped everyone find their voice while making sure each story fit into Microsoft's bigger picture.

The results were remarkable. Under Satya Nadella's leadership, and with Clayton's storytelling guidance, Microsoft's stock price tripled. More importantly, they shifted from being seen as tech's old guard to becoming a leader in cloud computing and artificial intelligence.

But here's what most people miss: Clayton's success wasn't just about being a good storyteller. It was about his ability to coordinate and amplify the voices of thousands of Microsoft employees while maintaining a consistent, compelling narrative.

What Does a Content Manager Actually Do?

A content manager is the in-house owner of a company's content marketing initiatives.

They are accountable for getting content done—and getting it done right. They drive traffic, leads and sales through consistent, high-quality content that builds trust with your audience.

We all deal with the challenge of creating consistent, valuable content. The quality of your marketing often depends on having someone dedicated to this craft.

The three core responsibilities of a content conductor are:

1. **Strategic leadership:** Setting the vision, creating the strategy, defining goals, allocating resources, measuring performance and evolving your content programme.

2. **Tactical coordination:** Overseeing production, controlling quality, managing the team, improving processes, implementing tools and designing workflows.

3. **Cultural facilitation:** Perhaps the most overlooked aspect of content leadership. The secret to lasting results isn't just producing great content once, but building a system that continuously improves your content operation.

But here's the most important quality: the right candidate will have more than just hard skills.

They will have the heart of a teacher, with a love of learning, writing and communicating in all forms.

They will see the value of every person on your team and put them at ease, empowering them to tell their stories to your audience.

You'll be surprised how many potential content manager candidates seem to have the right qualifications on paper. They come from a communications or journalism background, have an impeccable command of the English language, and thrive in fast-paced, deadline-driven environments.

Still, they will fail in the role if they do not embody its core spirit.

Someone either has the heart of a teacher, or they don't. And if they don't, it doesn't matter how qualified they might otherwise seem they will never be a successful content manager.

Why You Can't Just Divide Content Tasks Among Your Teams

You might be wondering, "Can't I just divide content responsibilities among my existing team?"

News flash: **content is a full-time job**.

It takes time to plan, write, edit, publish, distribute and analyse.

When you tack content onto an already full plate of responsibilities, it's often the first thing to fall off the back burner and not get done. Believe me, I've seen it happen all too frequently.

Someone needs to oversee making sure this doesn't happen—and be empowered to ensure it doesn't.

That's your content manager.

Changes that seem small and unimportant at first will compound into remarkable results if you're willing to stick with them for years. A dedicated content manager is that seemingly small change that compounds over time.

Start As You Mean To Go On

Let's return to Microsoft's transformation. Steve Clayton's success is a prime example of orchestrating a content operation that could consistently produce great content at scale.

The result? Microsoft didn't just tell a better story—they became a better story. Their market value grew from £300 billion to over £1 trillion, but more importantly, they rebuilt trust with their audience.

Why? Because their content was well-produced and well-conducted.

Every action you take in building a content team is a vote for the type of marketing business you wish to become, and a step towards investing to make it successful.

Chapter Summary

- Even with enthusiastic team members, content marketing needs someone dedicated to orchestrating strategy.

- Microsoft's transformation illustrates this perfectly. Appointing Steve Clayton as Chief Storyteller helped shift their image from outdated to innovative, while tripling their stock price.

- A content manager owns three core responsibilities: strategic leadership (setting vision and goals), tactical coordination (overseeing production), and cultural facilitation (building systems for continuous improvement).

- The right candidate needs more than technical qualifications. They must have the heart of a teacher, with a love of learning and communication, to empower others to tell their stories.

- Content creation can't be effectively divided among existing team members as secondary responsibilities. It requires dedicated focus to ensure it doesn't fall to the bottom of priorities.

CHAPTER 49

Success Factor 3: Leveraging In-House Subject Matter Experts

Stop the press. You don't need to hire more writers.

This is the first instinct when businesses are struggling with content marketing. Meanwhile, they're sitting on a plethora of expertise that could transform their content strategy.

Let me give an example. In 2015, Drift was just another marketing software company in a crowded market. They had a blog, social media presence and all the usual content marketing tactics. But something was missing—their content wasn't moving the needle.

Then they made a crucial discovery: their VP of Sales, David Cancel, wasn't just good at selling—he was a natural storyteller with deep insights into conversational marketing. Instead of having marketing write about sales concepts, they put Cancel behind a microphone.

The result? Their *Seeking Wisdom* podcast exploded, generating over two million blog views annually. But here's what most people miss about this story: the content was always there, locked inside Cancel's head. They just needed the right system to extract and share it.

Every action you take in creating systems to unlock this expertise is a vote for the type of marketing organisation you wish to become.

Everyone Can Be a Part of Your Content Marketing

While traditional sales and marketing activities are handled by specialised teams, it doesn't have to stop there.

The employee who is providing a service, manufacturing a product, or sending out an invoice is interacting, either directly or indirectly, with a customer or potential customer.

In this way, **they are part of your marketing and sales efforts**. Good customer experiences create happy customers, which, in turn, create enthusiastic promoters and more prospective customers.

This is happening every second of every day. The marketplace is constantly forming and refining its impression of your brand, and a positive experience makes all the difference.

How can we design a world where it's easy for these team members to contribute to content? That's where the role of Subject Matter Expert comes in.

What Makes a Great Subject Matter Expert?

At its core, being a Subject Matter Expert (SME) for your content team means being willing to share your knowledge and insights to help create content that truly answers your customers' questions.

These SMEs could be sales professionals, product designers, customer service experts, or company leaders—anyone with knowledge and authority on the issue at hand.

The way most subject matter experts help with content production is by being interviewed by content managers.

Think of your content manager as a reporter for your company. They need to write the content that will drive traffic and capture leads, but they don't have the first-hand knowledge to do so.

Therefore, they interview SMEs to get the information they need, which they can then shape into a full-fledged piece of content. One 20-minute meeting can turn into a multitude of article types, such as:

- **Articles with input**: An article that quotes the SME as the expert and uses information from the interview to specifically address the topic at hand.

- **Q&A-type articles**: A published interview that includes the content manager's questions and the SME's answers. This works best for questions with short answers.

- **Ghostwritten articles**: Depending on your company's needs, your content manager may write and publish as the SME, particularly if they are a C-level executive. Ghostwritten content can help build the brand and establish the voice of busy executives.

Content managers can't do it all on their own. They need team members from other departments to step up and share their expertise so that they can share that expertise with your audience.

The more team members who share, the more effective your content marketing will be.

If no one is willing to help, it will die on the vine.

So, how can you be the best SME possible?

First off, **you need to be willing**. If your content manager approaches you or sends a message asking for an interview, respond positively.

Even better, you can volunteer to help with a particular piece of content. If they're writing something bigger, like a buyer's guide or pillar page, they might need a good deal of help. Be willing to serve as their go-to expert when they have questions.

If you're a company leader, your willingness will encourage others to do the same. By contrast, your hesitancy will signal that content marketing is not really a priority.

Second, **challenge yourself to enjoy the process**. Your content manager might be a newer employee, maybe even a young professional who's eager but not yet polished. Help put them at ease by being invested in the project.

Even a small gesture of boredom letting out a sigh, checking your watch, glancing at your email can destroy their confidence and make them feel like they're deeply inconveniencing you.

Not only will this damage the employee's morale, it will also hurt your organisation's content marketing initiative.

Third, **offer specific feedback**. The editing process should feel collaborative. Posting a comment that says "I don't like this part" does little to improve the content or your relationship with the content manager. Instead, say, "I'm not sure about this part. The phrasing feels too biased. What do you think?"

Finally, when you serve as an SME for your content manager, you're giving the most noteworthy support you can for your content marketing initiative. **This is leading by example, and the effect is enormous**.

Make sure others at your company know that you took part and that you enjoyed the process. Tell others how easy it was. Talk to leadership and compliment the content manager. Share the post on LinkedIn. Celebrate the content wins, however small.

Every action you take further normalises the process and builds momentum for future content marketing plans.

Your Content is a Team Effort

Content creation requires structure, but it also requires the right culture behind it. It won't happen smoothly if your employees aren't encouraged to make time for it.

If you are ready to put content production at the centre of your marketing strategy, make sure the whole company is ready for such a change.

If not, the greatest content manager in the world will struggle.

Chapter Summary

- Companies often overlook their existing internal expertise while seeking more writers. This is demonstrated by Drift discovering their VP of Sales, David Cancel's storytelling ability, which led to a podcast generating two million blog views annually.

- Subject Matter Experts (SMEs) exist throughout your organisation. From product designers to customer service representatives, each has valuable knowledge that can be transformed into compelling content.

- Content managers function as company reporters, interviewing SMEs to create three main content types: articles with expert input (80%), Q&A-style pieces (10%), and ghostwritten executive content.

- Being an effective SME requires four key behaviours: willingness to participate when asked, genuine enthusiasm during the process, providing specific constructive feedback, and celebrating content wins publicly.

- Content creation requires both structure and the right supportive culture. Without company-wide encouragement to make time for content production, even the most talented content manager will struggle.

CHAPTER 50

Success Factor 4: The Balance of Quality AND Quantity in Content Production

"Do you want it done fast or done right?"

This false dichotomy has plagued content marketing since its inception. But here's the truth: you need both quality and quantity to succeed—just not in the way most people think.

The Inevitable Flood

Cast your mind back to 2012.

Content marketing was the new darling of digital strategy, and agencies had a simple prescription: "**Just publish more content!**"

Like eager students, businesses followed this advice. Marketing teams raced to fill editorial calendars. Blog sections grew exponentially. Content production became a numbers game, with success measured by publishing frequency rather than audience impact.

Fast forward to today, and we're drowning in content. Every minute sees:

- 500+ hours of video uploaded to YouTube

- 1,000+ articles published on WordPress

- 347,000+ new stories shared on Instagram

With everyone following the "more is better" playbook, **we've created a deafening digital noise that makes it increasingly difficult to stand out**, rank in search results, or even be noticed.

History Repeats with AI

Just when we thought we'd learned our lesson, history is repeating itself with AI-generated content.

The arrival of ChatGPT and similar tools has triggered another mad rush of quantity over quality.

"Just ask AI to write your blogs!" is the new "just publish more content!"

Don't misunderstand me. I won't dismiss using AI in your content production process (we'll explore this in Chapter 58). But we've reached a tipping point where businesses are lazily churning out AI-generated content without strategic direction or human refinement.

The result? Another flood of mediocre content that sounds remarkably similar, lacks a distinctive perspective, and fails to genuinely serve audiences.

The moral of the story? You do not rise to the level of your goals. You fall to the level of your systems.

Finding the True Balance

This brings us back to the age-old debate of "quality versus quantity." How can we design a world where content cuts through, rather than contributes to, the noise?

I'm here to tell you that framing it as an either/or question misses the point entirely. Both matter—just not in the ways most people think.

Why Quality Matters More Than Ever

Search engines have grown increasingly sophisticated. Google's helpful content update explicitly rewards content that:

- Demonstrates first-hand expertise

- Offers genuine insights and analysis

- Provides substantial value to readers

Beyond Google, remember our earlier discussion about diversifying your content distribution. Quality content performs better across platforms because it:

- Earns social shares and backlinks organically

- Encourages deeper engagement and time spent

- Builds genuine trust with your audience

- Converts better at every stage of the funnel

Every piece of mediocre content you publish diminishes your brand's perceived expertise, trustworthiness and authority.

Why Quantity Still Matters

Despite the obvious importance of quality, quantity still plays a vital role.

Sufficient content volume is needed to gain initial traction—meaning more quality content creates more entry points for your audience. Regular publishing maintains audience expectation and engagement, creating a consistent output that signals reliability and provides your business with staying power.

The secret to getting results that last is to never stop making improvements to your content balance.

The HubSpot Wake-Up Call

HubSpot's experience perfectly illustrates this balance. In early 2025, HubSpot faced a dramatic crisis that went viral across social media: reports claiming they had lost 80% of their blog traffic seemingly overnight.

For a company whose brand was built on content marketing excellence, this sparked widespread speculation about "the end of SEO" and even "the downfall of HubSpot's core strategy."

But as Kieran Flanagan, one of the architects of HubSpot's SEO strategy, later explained, the reality was far more nuanced—and a warning for all content marketers to heed.

What happened? HubSpot had begun shifting their content approach years earlier, around 2020, when they noticed Google increasingly rewarding influence rather than just information. Instead of chasing traffic volume with broad informational content, they strategically:

1. Invested in channels like YouTube, podcasts and social media

2. Built out HubSpot Academy for deeper educational content

3. Acquired The Hustle to strengthen their founder-centric approach

4. Focused on depth and expertise rather than content breadth

The results were a complete transformation of their content operation that delivered:

- Strong performance for transactional keywords (which actually grew substantially)

- Better visibility in AI-generated responses from tools like ChatGPT

- More qualified leads from their most relevant content

- Sustained influence with both human readers and AI systems

What's crucial to understand is that HubSpot didn't abandon content marketing—they optimised it. They found their ideal approach by focusing on depth over breadth, expertise over volume, and influence over mere information.

Finding Your Sweet Spot

The "right" balance of quality and quantity varies for every business based on factors such as your audience's needs and consumption habits, your industry's content saturation level, and how much capacity and expertise you have available.

Instead of asking, "How much content should we publish?" set yourself minimum thresholds, as well as an optimal publishing frequency. In doing so, you can determine the best ways to maximise the impact of each piece of content you publish.

Changes that seem small and unimportant at first will compound into remarkable results if you're willing to stick with them for years.

Here are some other tips to consider:

1. Define Your Quality Standards

Create clear guidelines for what constitutes quality in your content:

- Research requirements (original research, expert interviews, data analysis)

- Writing standards (voice, style, structure, technical accuracy)

- Value thresholds (what specific value must each piece provide?)

- SEO requirements (on-page elements, semantic relevance, intent matching)

2. Design Your Production System

Build a process that balances efficiency with excellence:

- Realistic editorial calendars based on team capacity

- Templates and frameworks that speed production without sacrificing quality

- Clear workflows with adequate time for research, writing and editing

- Resource allocation that matches content importance

3. Measure What Matters

Track metrics that reveal true content performance:

- Engagement metrics (time on page, scroll depth, comments)

- Conversion metrics (downloads, sign-ups, sales)

- SEO performance (rankings, organic traffic, featured snippets)

- Long-term impact (backlinks, repeated visits, brand mentions)

Fight the Flood

As AI-generated content floods the market, the bar for standing out will only rise higher.

The businesses that thrive won't be those producing the most content—or even the "best" content in isolation. They'll be those that find their optimal balance between quality and quantity.

Don't think of it as choosing quality over quantity. Instead, think about how to optimise both for maximum impact.

- The content marketing landscape has evolved from the 2012 "publish more content" approach to today's overwhelming digital noise, with history repeating through AI-generated content.

- Quality content has become essential as search engines reward first-hand expertise, genuine insights and substantial value, while poor content diminishes brand authority.

- Quantity still matters for gaining initial traction, maintaining audience engagement and creating multiple entry points for your audience.

- HubSpot's experience shows the importance of strategic balance. They maintained success by focusing on depth over breadth, expertise over volume and influence over mere information.

- Find your optimal balance by defining clear quality standards, designing efficient production systems and measuring meaningful metrics rather than vanity numbers.

CHAPTER 51

Success Factor 5: Using Content to Transform Your Sales Process

How many pages of information would you be willing to read before making your decision? Ten? Twenty?

What about thirty?

If you're raising an eyebrow at that last number, stick with me. We're about to dive into the world of Assignment Selling, and trust me, those thirty pages are going to make a lot more sense soon.

There's a cry heard all too often from marketing teams: they're frustrated that their carefully crafted content sits unused by sales.

Yet the most successful companies I work with have discovered something remarkable: using content doesn't add time to the sales process— it dramatically reduces it.

Let's start with a story about our old friend, Marcus Sheridan. You remember Marcus, right? The pool guy who saved his business with a single article about pricing?

Well, he's back, and he's about to show us the power of Assignment Selling. It's exactly what it sounds like: assigning prospects "homework" before your sales interactions.

For example, in the old days at River Pools and Spas, a typical customer interaction might go something like this:

"Hey Marcus, I'm checking out your website. Could you come out to my house this Friday and give me a quote for a pool?"

And Marcus would say: "Sure!"

Simple, right?

But here's the problem: Marcus had no idea how educated (or uneducated) the customer was about pools. He was walking into an appointment blind, ready to spend hours explaining the basics before even getting to the quote.

It might sound counterintuitive. After all, won't asking prospects to read a thirty-page guide before a meeting scare them away?

The truth is quite the opposite. Requiring prospects to educate themselves does two powerful things:

1. It qualifies your leads by separating serious buyers from casual browsers

2. It shortens your sales cycle by addressing common questions upfront

Every action you take to educate prospects is a vote for the type of company you wish to become one that leads with value rather than pressure.

Assignment Selling in Action

Now, let's fast forward to the era of Assignment Selling. The conversation starts the same way, but Marcus's response? That's where things get interesting.

Marcus: "Sure, I'd love to! But..."

That "but" is where the magic happens. It's the gateway to Assignment Selling. Let's break down what Marcus does next:

1. He acknowledges the significance of the purchase: "You're getting ready to spend a lot of money, and I know you don't want to make any mistakes."

2. He positions himself as a guide: "I'm going to make sure you're well educated."

3. He sets the stage for the assignment: "Here's what's going to happen. As we're talking on the phone right now, I'm going to send you two things that you're going to love."

The first part of Marcus's assignment is a video. But it's not just any video. It's a comprehensive look at the entire pool installation process. Why is this important?

1. **It saves time**: before assignment selling, a typical appointment would take about two and a half hours. This video alone saves thirty minutes of explanation time.

2. **It sets expectations**: the customer knows exactly what to expect during the installation process.

3. **It builds trust**: by showing the entire process, warts and all, Marcus is demonstrating transparency and confidence in his work.

Now we come to the magic number: the thirty-page guide.

Yes, you read that right.

Thirty. Pages.

But before you baulk at the length, listen to how Marcus presents it:

"This guide is great because it's going to answer a lot of the questions that you have, or that you should have, that nobody has addressed yet."

He then gives examples of what the guide covers: types of heaters, pool covers, and more. He's not just dumping information on the customer; he's addressing specific concerns and questions they might not even know they have yet.

And here's the kicker: "Now this guide, it's a little bit long it's about... thirty pages but I promise, it will be well worth your time."

When Marcus Sheridan implemented this at River Pools and Spas, their sales cycle shortened by 75%, and their closing rate soared to 95%.

Content wasn't just marketing material it became an integral part of their sales process.

The Commitment: The Key to Success

Now, here's where most people get it wrong. They might say something like, "Hey, I'm going to send you a video. It'd be great if you could give it a look."

That's not selling. That's hoping.

Real assignment selling is when you clearly explain what you're sending, why it matters, and what the customer will miss out on if they don't engage with it. And then and this is crucial you get a commitment.

Marcus doesn't ask, "How does that sound to you?" because the response to that is usually a non-committal "Fine." And "fine" doesn't mean anything.

Instead, he asks for a clear commitment: "Will you take the time to do these things before our appointment on Friday?"

Let's look at an example you could use when prospects first reach out, whether that's having filled out a form or making a call. In this example, our goal is to immediately send them relevant content that addresses their likely questions. This message might sound something like:

"Hi Sarah! Thanks for reaching out about our services. I'm looking forward to our call next Wednesday.

I've attached a guide that will answer your initial questions and explain the options you should consider. This way, when we meet, we can focus specifically on your unique needs instead of covering basics.

If you can't read this before our meeting, let me know and we'll reschedule for a better time. Can you confirm you'll review this before Wednesday?"

Did you notice the "what", "why" and "when"? This approach works because:

- We have clearly explained what the "assignment" is

- We have previewed why the "assignment" matters

- We have established when it needs to be completed

Most importantly, we have asked for a commitment, ensuring they do it.

Let's talk about why this works. It comes back to the Zero Moment of Truth (ZMOT) we talked about earlier.

By providing this in-depth information upfront, you're not just educating your prospect. **You're actively participating in that crucial 80% of their decision-making process**.

You're shaping their understanding of the product and your company before they ever set foot in your store or have a face-to-face meeting.

The secret to getting results that last is to never stop making improvements to how you integrate content into sales. Doing this makes your time more productive and helps them understand their options instead of going in blind.

"But What About People Who Say 'No'?"

This is a completely natural fear for a lot of sales reps when first discovering Assignment Selling: what happens when prospects refuse to do their homework?

Believe it or not, this is a gift, because it tells you something crucial about them.

If someone isn't willing to invest time in understanding their purchase, they're likely making decisions based primarily on price rather than value. They're probably not your ideal customer.

You might respond with: "This material will help prevent you from making common mistakes and will make our time together much more productive. But if you can't review it, that's okay. It likely means we aren't the right fit for each other."

Remember: **selling is a partnership**. You're the educator, helping prospects make the best decision for their needs. If they won't invest in learning, they're not investing in the relationship.

The most effective form of learning is practice, not planning. Train your sales team to practise this approach until it becomes second nature.

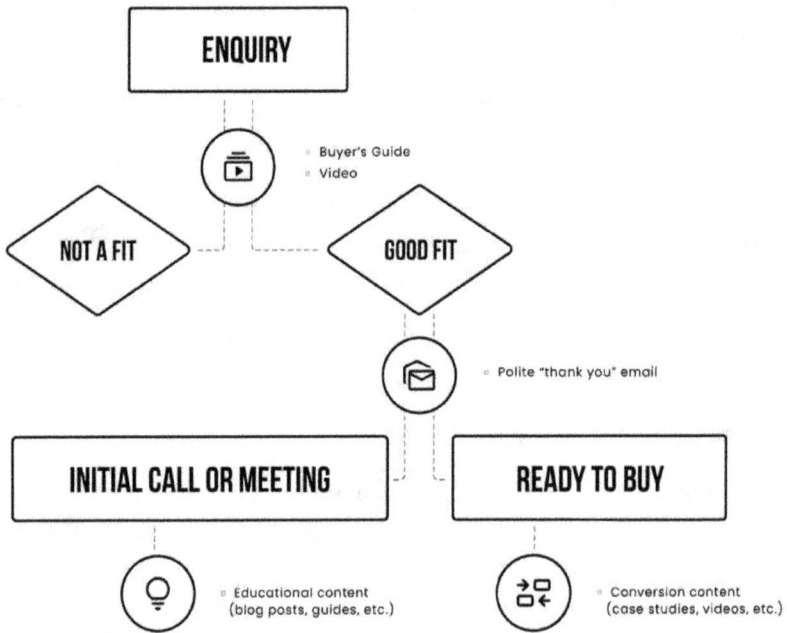

Assignment Selling Beyond the First Contact

One mistake businesses make is thinking Assignment Selling is just for the initial contact or the start of the sales process.

But it's much more than that. For it to work effectively, you need a clear system for which content to send at each stage of the sales process.

Content for the first contact is best used to answer high-level questions. Focus on addressing the fundamentals that every prospect needs to understand.

After that initial engagement, prospects move to the second stage and typically fall into three categories:

- **Not a good fit**: send a polite message that thanks them and leaves the door open

- **Maybe interested**: provide content that further educates and moves them down the funnel

- **Ready to buy**: send materials that facilitate the purchase decision

As they move to the third contact stage, by this point they are either not a fit or ready to buy. Your content should either gracefully end the relationship or make the purchase process clear and simple.

The impact of assignment selling is profound:

1. **Shorter sales cycles**: instead of spending hours explaining basics, you can focus on specific needs.

2. **More qualified leads**: prospects who complete their "homework" demonstrate real commitment.

3. **Higher close rates**: educated customers make confident decisions more quickly.

4. **Measurable ROI**: companies have tracked hundreds of thousands in revenue directly tied to specific content pieces.

Changes that seem small and unimportant at first will compound into remarkable results if you're willing to stick with them for years.

Making It Work in Your Business

To successfully implement assignment selling, remember these four principles:

1. **Train until it's automatic**: your sales team needs to be comfortable with the process until it becomes second nature

2. **Create truly valuable content**: the assignments must genuinely answer prospects' questions and address concerns

3. **Track and measure results**: monitor which content pieces lead to closed deals and continuously refine

4. **Get team buy-in**: have regular meetings where sales and marketing discuss which assignments work best at each stage

Remember that today's buyers crave education. By providing in-depth information upfront, you're not just educating prospects. You're actively participating in their decision-making process, shaping their understanding of both your solution and your company.

Honest and transparent content is the greatest sales and trust-building tool in the world. It's not just about marketing; it's about empowering your sales team and your buyers with the resources they need to succeed.

Sales needs content as much as content needs sales. They're two sides of the same coin, working together to create informed, confident customers who are ready to buy.

The specific approaches and content types may vary, but the principle remains: content is your greatest sales tool.

So, ask yourself this: how can you design a world where your content naturally becomes part of your prospect's buying process?

- Assignment Selling involves giving prospects "homework" before sales interactions. This qualifies serious buyers and shortens the sales cycle, as seen when River Pools and Spas achieved a 95% closing rate.

- Effective assignments include three key elements: explaining why the material matters, previewing what value they'll receive, and establishing how important it is to complete it.

- Prospects who refuse to do the homework reveal themselves as likely price-focused rather than value-focused, a gift that helps identify less suitable customers early.

- Create a clear system for which content to send at each sales stage— from answering fundamentals during first contact to facilitating purchase decisions in later interactions.

- Train your sales team until the process becomes second nature, create truly valuable content, track which pieces lead to closed deals, and ensure marketing and sales collaborate on effective assignments.

CHAPTER 52

Success Factor 6: Measure, Test, and Optimise

One of the tragedies that often befalls marketers working in-house is the difficulty in measuring the impact of their content. I had this same problem myself early in my career.

Though it reveals a fundamental misunderstanding of modern content marketing, the truth is, you absolutely can measure content performance.

More importantly, you must.

In 2015, Moz (then SEOmoz) was struggling with a problem many content marketers would love to have. They had plenty of traffic, but disappointing conversion rates.

Despite having industry-leading content that attracted thousands of visitors daily, they weren't turning those visitors into customers at the rate they needed. Then they partnered with conversion rate experts to implement a rigorous measurement and testing programme.

The result?

A staggering 170% increase in conversion rates.

But here's what most people miss about this story: it wasn't creativity or design that drove this success. It was methodical measurement, hypothesis testing and data-driven optimisation.

Building Your Measurement Framework

We all deal with the challenge of proving content marketing ROI. One of the main issues is that marketers often focus on vanity metrics. Whilst these are important, they don't give you everything you need to prove the worth of your content marketing efforts.

Effective content measurement starts with identifying what truly matters to your business. Instead of drowning in data, focus on these four categories of metrics that tell the complete story:

1. Traffic Metrics

These reveal content discovery and reach:

- Organic traffic growth
- Referral sources
- Search visibility
- Social amplification

2. Engagement Metrics

These show content resonance and quality:

- Time on page
- Scroll depth
- Comments and shares
- Return visits

3. Conversion Metrics

These demonstrate content effectiveness:

- Email sign-ups

- Content downloads

- Demo requests

- Free trial starts

4. Revenue Metrics

These prove business impact:

- Pipeline influence

- Closed deals

- Customer acquisition cost

- Content ROI

The key is connecting these metrics to create a clear story of how content drives business results.

HubSpot did exactly this when they analysed their historical content performance data, discovering that comprehensive pillar pages significantly outperformed standard blog posts.

This insight led them to restructure their content strategy around pillar content, resulting in a 50% increase in organic traffic.

They didn't guess. They measured, learned and adapted.

The Testing Methodology That Works

Simply measuring performance isn't enough. You need a systematic approach to testing improvements, and different situations call for different testing methods.

The four tests that I think are most important to be running repeatedly are:

- **A/B testing**: perfect for comparing two versions of the same content element (headlines, calls to action, images)

- **Multivariate testing**: ideal for understanding how multiple variables interact to impact performance

- **User testing**: essential for gaining qualitative insights into how people interact with your content

- **Content experiments**: these broader tests compare different content approaches, formats or strategies

But measuring and testing is only half the battle. A lot of marketers stop there, but the ones who see real results will optimise based on the data they find.

By testing and analysing, **you're able to use your content metrics to identify both top performers and underperformers**. This will help pinpoint specific elements that could deliver the biggest performance gains.

Once you've got that, focus on high-impact, low-effort improvements first to build momentum, and then direct your time and budget to the areas with the greatest potential return.

Rinse and repeat. The secret to getting results that last is to never stop making improvements based on what you learn.

Measure, Test, Optimise

The quality of your content marketing results depends on the quality of your measurement systems.

Let's return to the Moz success story. Their 170% conversion rate improvement didn't happen overnight or through a single test. It was the result of a committed, systematic approach to measurement and optimisation.

Their success, like that of every business that excels at content marketing, came from transforming measurement from an occasional activity into a core discipline.

If you take the same approach, you'll see your content marketing go from a creative exercise into a predictable, scalable business driver.

Chapter Summary

- Effective content measurement is possible and essential, as demonstrated by Moz's 170% conversion rate increase through methodical testing rather than simply relying on creativity.

- Focus on four key metric categories: traffic metrics (organic growth, referral sources), engagement metrics (time on page, scroll depth), conversion metrics (sign-ups, downloads), and revenue metrics (pipeline influence, closed deals).

- Implement systematic testing approaches including A/B testing for comparing content elements, multivariate testing for understanding interactions, and user testing for qualitative insights.

- Use your measurement data to identify both top performers and underperformers, then prioritise high-impact, low-effort improvements before tackling larger optimisations.

- Make measurement a core discipline. Successful content marketing requires continuous testing and refinement rather than a one-time effort.

PART 4

Making It Work: Practical Tips for Implementation

CHAPTER 53

Putting Your Trust BLUEPRINT^{TM} Into Action

You've learned the principles.

You understand the strategy.

Now comes the hard part: implementing these ideas in your actual business.

In the chapters ahead, we'll explore the practical side of everything you've learnt, giving you the tools, team structures, and frameworks you need to turn theory into results.

First, we'll tackle the technology question. With over 8,000 marketing tools available, choosing the right systems can feel overwhelming. You'll discover whether an all-in-one platform like HubSpot or a custom-built "Frankenspot" makes more sense for your situation, based on your budget, team size, and growth plans.

Next, we'll examine how to build a marketing team that drives real growth. Starting with a Content Manager as your foundation, you'll learn how to expand your capabilities in phases—from a small foundational team to a fully scaled marketing function.

For businesses not ready to build a full in-house team, we'll explore smarter approaches to external support.

You'll learn why the traditional agency model often creates harmful dependency and discover alternatives like coaching-focused partners and fractional leadership that build your capabilities rather than just delivering temporary results.

We'll then look at futureproofing your content strategy in a rapidly changing landscape. From the AI revolution to the rise of YouTube as the "University of Everything" and the growing importance of voice search, you'll understand how to generate the trust signals that will matter most in the coming years.

Finally, we'll show you how to prove your content's worth through robust ROI measurement.

Companies that consistently track content performance are 12 times more likely to see year-on-year growth in returns. You'll learn to balance direct revenue metrics with indirect value indicators and build attribution models that connect content to real business outcomes.

Throughout these chapters, you'll find practical frameworks, real-world examples, and actionable steps to implement immediately.

Whether you lead a small business looking to build trust on a budget or a larger company transforming your approach to marketing, these tools will help you create sustainable systems for growth.

The strategies in this book aren't theoretical.

They're battle-tested approaches used by businesses of all sizes to build trust, shorten sales cycles, and drive sustainable growth.

Now it's time to put them into action in your business.

Are you ready to build a marketing function that actually works?

CHAPTER 54

Tools of the Trade: Building Your Marketing Technology Foundation

After exploring the strategies and principles that build a trusted brand, it's time to address the practical side of implementation, which leads you to wonder, "What tools do I need to make all of this happen?"

It's a fair question.

You can have the best marketing strategy in the world, but without the right tools to execute it efficiently, you might find yourself overwhelmed and unable to measure what's working.

The marketing technology landscape has exploded in recent years. In 2011, there were about 150 marketing technology solutions available.

By 2022, that number had grown to over 8,000.

This abundance of choice can lead to decision paralysis or, worse, a cobbled-together system where your tools don't communicate with each other effectively.

During my career, I've noticed a pattern: companies with integrated systems consistently outperform those using disconnected tools.

When sales and marketing teams can see the same data and work from the same platform, trust builds between departments, leads are handled more effectively, and ROI becomes much easier to track.

The Power of an All-in-One Solution

Among all the tools I've worked with, one platform stands out as particularly effective for implementing the trust-building strategies we've discussed: **HubSpot**.

Let me be completely straightforward: HubSpot hasn't paid me to mention them in this book. I am a Certified Partner and receive commission when I sell a business a HubSpot licence, but my recommendation in this book comes purely from years of seeing clients transform their marketing efforts after adopting this platform.

What makes HubSpot so effective is its comprehensive approach. Rather than piecing together separate systems for your website, email marketing, social media, sales pipeline, and analytics, HubSpot brings everything under one roof in several main hubs that work together:

- **Marketing Hub**: This handles everything from email campaigns and social media posting to landing pages and automated workflows. The real magic happens when you can see how your marketing efforts directly translate to sales opportunities.

- **Sales Hub**: This provides tools for managing your pipeline, scheduling meetings, and tracking communications with prospects. Sales teams can see exactly which marketing content their prospects have engaged with, giving them valuable context for conversations.

- **Service Hub**: Once someone becomes a customer, this hub helps you deliver outstanding service through ticket management, knowledge bases, and customer feedback tools.

- **Content Hub**: This powers your website with templates optimised for conversion and tools that make updating content simple, even for non-technical users.

- **Operations Hub**: This powers your business operations by connecting your apps, syncing and cleaning customer data, and automating processes—all within one central CRM.

- **Commerce Hub**: This powers your business commerce by centralising payments, quotes, invoices, and subscriptions, letting you manage the entire quote-to-cash process, automate billing, and track revenue.

This integration creates three significant advantages. First, your data stays consistent across all functions. Second, your teams can collaborate more effectively. Most importantly, you can track a customer's entire journey from first touch to final sale.

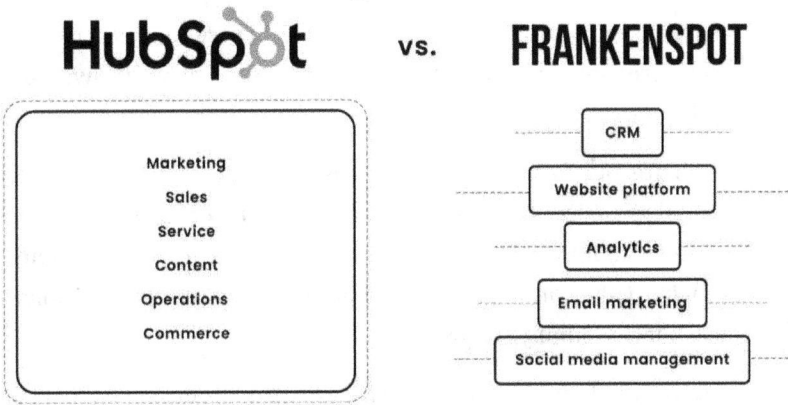

Building Your Own "Frankenspot"

Despite its advantages, I recognise that HubSpot isn't the right fit for every business.

You might have budget constraints, specific needs that require specialised tools, or existing systems that you're not ready to replace.

If that's your situation, you can still create an effective marketing technology stack by carefully selecting individual tools that work well together—what some marketers jokingly call a *"Frankenspot"*, a term coined by HubSpot itself.

Building your own tech stack requires more planning and maintenance, but it can be just as effective if done thoughtfully.

The key is choosing tools that integrate well with each other and limiting yourself to only what you truly need.

For most businesses implementing the trust-building strategies we've discussed, a basic "Frankenspot" might include:

- **CRM system**: The foundation of your stack should be a solid customer relationship management system. Salesforce remains the market leader with incredible customisation options, though it can be complex to implement. For smaller businesses, options like Keap (formerly Infusionsoft) offer good functionality at a lower price point.

- **Website platform**: Your website is often the centrepiece of your digital presence. WordPress powers over 40% of all websites on the internet, offering incredible flexibility and a huge ecosystem of plugins. Other options like Duda or Squarespace can be simpler to use but may limit your growth.

- **Analytics**: Understanding your website traffic and user behaviour is vital. Google Analytics remains the standard choice here, giving you deep insights into how visitors find and interact with your content.

- **Email marketing**: Your email platform should make it easy to segment your audience and create personalised content journeys. Mailchimp offers a user-friendly starting point, while ActiveCampaign provides more advanced automation capabilities as you grow.

- **Social media management**: Tools like Hootsuite, Buffer, or Sprinklr help you schedule content across multiple platforms and monitor engagement, saving countless hours of manual posting.

- **Sales enablement**: Platforms like Salesloft can help your sales team stay organised with sequence templates, call recording, and analysis to improve their effectiveness.

- **Meeting scheduling**: Simple tools like Calendly eliminate the back-and-forth of finding meeting times, making it frictionless for prospects to connect with your team.

The challenge with this approach is ensuring these separate systems can share data effectively.

Before investing in any tool, be sure to check that it integrates with existing systems and understand how data can flow between that tool and others.

Crucially, it's important to make sure that your "Frankenspot" system doesn't become a hindrance to teams.

In other words, will it create new silos or break down existing ones?

Making Your Choice

Whether you opt for an all-in-one solution like HubSpot or build your own technology stack, the right choice ultimately depends on your specific situation. Consider these factors:

- **Budget**: All-in-one platforms typically require a larger upfront investment but may save money in the long run through efficiency gains and reduced integration costs.

- **Team Size**: Smaller teams often benefit more from integrated platforms that reduce the administrative burden, while larger businesses might have dedicated staff for each marketing function.

- **Technical Resources**: Building and maintaining your own stack requires more technical expertise, either in-house or through consultants.

- **Growth Plans**: If you anticipate significant growth, choose solutions that can scale with you to avoid painful migrations later.

Remember that even the best tools are only as effective as the strategy behind them. A mediocre tool in the hands of a skilled marketer will outperform the most sophisticated platform used without clear purpose.

The tools you choose should support your trust-building efforts, not define them. They should make it easier to create valuable content, maintain consistent communication, track your progress, and deliver excellent customer experiences.

Start with your strategy, then find the tools that enable it—not the other way around.

When in doubt, begin with the simplest solution that meets your needs, and evolve your technology as your marketing matures.

With the right tools supporting your trust-building efforts, you'll be well-equipped to serve your ideal clients for years to come.

Chapter Summary

- The marketing technology landscape has expanded from 150 solutions in 2011 to over 8,000 by 2022. Companies with integrated systems consistently outperform those using disconnected tools.

- All-in-one platforms like HubSpot offer comprehensive solutions through connected hubs (Marketing, Sales, Service, Content, Operations, and Commerce) that track the entire customer journey within one system.

- For businesses needing alternative solutions, building a "Frankenspot" requires careful selection of tools that integrate well, including CRM, website platform, analytics, email marketing, and social media management.

- When choosing between all-in-one or custom solutions, consider your budget, team size, technical resources, and growth plans to determine which approach best supports your specific situation.

- Remember that tools should support your trust-building strategy rather than define it. Start with your strategy first, then select the simplest technology that meets your needs and can evolve as your marketing matures.

Reader's Resource: Curious about implementing an all-in-one marketing solution for your business?

Scan this QR code to explore HubSpot's platform and discover if it's the right fit for your needs.

CHAPTER 55

Scaling Up: Assembling The Right Marketing Team

Growing your marketing function isn't just about hiring bodies to fill seats.

It's about building a team that can transform your business through strategic, consistent, and authentic communication with your audience.

When done right, your marketing team becomes the engine that powers sustainable growth for your entire business.

As we covered in Chapter 48, your first marketing hire should be a Content Manager. **This role is vital because content forms the foundation of all your marketing efforts.**

A good Content Manager doesn't just write blog posts. They develop a comprehensive strategy that answers your customers' questions at every stage of their journey. They should have:

- Strong writing skills across multiple formats.

- The ability to understand your customer's questions and pain points.

- A strategic mindset for planning content that supports your business goals.

- Basic SEO knowledge.

- Project management capabilities.

With this role filled, you can begin producing consistent, high-quality content that builds trust with your audience and serves as fuel for all your marketing channels.

The Natural Growth Progression

As your content foundation solidifies and your business grows, the next logical hire should be a Videographer. This might surprise some people who think of video as a "nice-to-have", but the data tells a different story.

According to Wyzowl's 2023 State of Video Marketing report, 91% of businesses use video as a marketing tool, and 87% of video marketers say video has increased traffic to their website[26].

More importantly, 94% of marketers say video has helped increase understanding of their product or service.

Your videographer will capture your company's personality and bring your products and services to life in ways text simply cannot. They'll create everything from customer testimonials to product demos, thought leadership interviews, and educational content.

After establishing your content creation team, the next critical hire is a Head of Marketing. This person will ultimately be responsible for leading the growing marketing team.

From there, your hiring should match your specific business needs:

- An SEO Specialist if organic search is a key channel.

- A Marketing Technologist if you need to optimise your tech stack.

- A Graphic Designer for stronger visual branding.

- A Social Media Manager for expanding your social presence.

- A Website Developer for ongoing site improvements.

However your team grows, **the heart of your marketing function should be authentic content creation.**

With a Content Manager and Videographer focused full-time on creating high-quality material, you'll have a steady stream of valuable assets to fuel your marketing efforts.

This approach works because today's buyers crave genuine, helpful information from trusted sources. By having dedicated content creators working closely with your sales team to address real customer questions, you establish that trust.

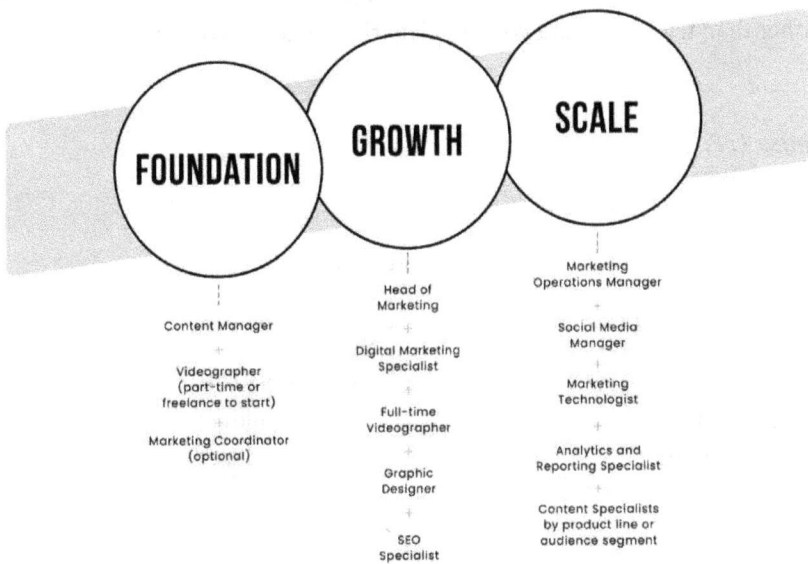

Building Your Team: A Phased Approach

Before making any hiring decisions, it's worth evaluating your current customer journey—from a prospect's first interaction through to becoming a loyal customer. Pay special attention to the marketing-sales handoff.

Ask yourself:

- Can prospects easily find answers to their questions on your website?

- Do your marketing materials educate buyers or just promote your products?

- How do leads describe their experience with your sales team?

- Where do prospects get stuck or drop out of your funnel?

This audit will reveal gaps in your customer experience that can guide your hiring priorities.

From there, consider this phased approach based on business stage, rather than trying to build your ideal marketing team overnight:

Phase 1: Foundation (1–3 people)

- Content Manager

- Videographer (part-time or freelance to start)

- Marketing Coordinator (optional)

At this stage, you want to focus on **establishing your content foundation**, creating valuable resources for your audience, and developing basic processes.

Phase 2: Growth (4–7 people)

- Head of Marketing

- Full-time Videographer

- SEO Specialist

- Graphic Designer

- Digital Marketing Specialist

This is the phase in which you **expand your content creation capabilities** by adding specialist skills to improve distribution and performance.

Sometimes this is also a result of natural attrition. When team members leave or get promoted, you can use this as an opportunity to evaluate what skills and mindset you need in their replacement.

Use that to update job descriptions to reflect your vision for marketing's role in the business, and during interviews, clearly articulate your expectations for customer-focused, education-based marketing.

Phase 3: Scale (8+ people)

- Marketing Operations Manager
- Social Media Manager
- Marketing Technologist
- Content Specialists by product line or audience segment
- Analytics and Reporting Specialist

In the scaling phase, you're looking to add operational support and further specialisation to maintain quality while increasing output.

Take video production, for example. Many companies hire external agencies for occasional video projects, spending £10,000+ for a handful of videos that quickly become outdated.

By contrast, an in-house Videographer might cost £35,000 annually but can produce dozens of videos each month that continuously adapt to your evolving business.

Hiring Hurdles to Avoid

Many companies make the mistake of adding content creation responsibilities to already busy employees' plates.

This approach almost always fails because quality content requires dedicated focus.

When you hire roles like a Videographer or Content Manager, you're not just adding to your overhead. **You're investing in assets that will generate returns for years to come**.

Building a marketing team comes with other hurdles and mistakes. Pay attention to these:

- **Hiring too many specialists too early**: Without a strong content foundation, specialists won't have quality material to work with.

- **Prioritising quantity over quality**: Ten mediocre blog posts will never outperform three exceptional ones.

- **Neglecting team culture**: Marketing requires creativity and collaboration. Build a team that works well together.

- **Separating content creation from sales**: Your content creators should regularly meet with sales to understand customer questions.

- **Underinvesting in training**: Marketing is evolving rapidly. Budget for ongoing skill development.

Your Marketing Function Deserves a Seat at the Table

One of the biggest mistakes I've seen companies make is treating marketing as a support function rather than a strategic driver of business growth.

Your Head of Marketing, or whomever leads the team, must have a seat at the leadership table.

When marketing has proper representation in leadership discussions, you're able to align marketing initiatives with company-wide objectives.

But more importantly, marketing gets the resources it needs to drive growth, and the overall business better understands the role and value of your marketing function.

Remember, building a strong marketing team isn't just about generating leads. **It transforms how your entire business relates to customers.**

When done right, it becomes the voice of the customer throughout your business.

Your product team develops features customers want.

Your service team anticipates common questions.

Your sales team enters conversations with prospects who already trust your expertise.

This customer-centric approach creates a virtuous cycle: better understanding leads to more helpful content, which attracts more engaged prospects, who provide deeper insights, which improves your understanding further.

By investing in building a marketing team focused on authentic content creation and customer education, you're building a sustainable engine for business growth.

Chapter Summary

- The foundation of any effective marketing team begins with a Content Manager who can develop strategic content that addresses customer questions at each stage of their journey.

- Video content is not a luxury but a necessity, making a Videographer your second critical hire to bring your products and services to life in ways text cannot.

- Build your team in phases—starting with a foundation (1–3 people), moving to growth (4–7 people), and finally scaling (8+ people)— based on your business stage rather than attempting to create your ideal team overnight.

- Common pitfalls include adding content creation to already busy employees, hiring specialists too early, prioritising quantity over quality, and failing to connect content creation with sales insights.

- Your marketing function deserves representation at the leadership level to ensure alignment with company objectives and secure the resources needed to drive genuine business growth.

CHAPTER 56

Beyond Outsourcing: Finding the Right Marketing Support for Your Business

In the last chapter, we talked about the steps for building your marketing team.

That might sound ideal—after all, you'd have complete control, deep institutional knowledge, and people fully dedicated to your business.

But this path isn't always realistic.

You might face budget constraints that make hiring multiple full-time specialists impossible. Or perhaps you're in a location with a limited talent pool, making it hard to find the right people with the right skills.

When facing these challenges, many businesses automatically turn to marketing agencies.

It seems like the logical choice. After all, agencies offer specialised expertise, established processes, and the promise of results without having to manage a team yourself.

But is working with a traditional agency truly the best option?

Reframing the Agency—Client Relationship

I want to challenge this automatic thinking.

The standard agency relationship has become increasingly problematic in recent years.

To be clear, I'm not dismissing agencies entirely. They absolutely have their place in the marketing ecosystem. But the typical agency model often creates a fundamental issue: **dependency**.

Most agencies aren't incentivised to help you become self-sufficient. They want—and financially need—you to remain dependent on their services. This dependency can seriously limit your business growth in ways that aren't immediately obvious.

Take content creation, for instance. When an agency controls all your content, they're speaking for your business.

The problem? They'll never truly understand your company, your customers, or your industry the way you do.

This disconnect creates several problems that compound over time.

First, you miss countless opportunities to build genuine trust with your customers. When your content lacks the authentic voice and deep expertise that only comes from within your business, it feels generic.

Customers can sense this. They're looking for businesses that truly understand their problems and can speak to them directly—not through the filtered voice of an agency writer producing three blog posts a month.

Second, you end up spending money on temporary fixes rather than building lasting assets. Agency retainers typically cost thousands per month, often ranging from £3,000 to £15,000 or more.

What if you invested even a portion of that budget into developing your own marketing capabilities? Over time, the return would be significantly higher as you build internal skills that continue to deliver value year after year.

Third—and perhaps most devastating—**you surrender control over your growth trajectory**.

When you rely completely on an agency, you're always waiting for them to execute your vision. This creates inevitable delays and frustrations.

Even with the best agencies, there's a constant back-and-forth that slows down implementation. Simple projects can take weeks instead of days, and campaign launches get pushed back as you wait in the agency's queue behind other clients.

So, what's the solution?

Should you completely avoid agencies and try to do everything yourself despite limited resources?

Not at all.

The answer isn't to abandon outside help—**it's to evolve how you work with external partners**.

The Value of a Coach

Think about elite performers in any field. The best athletes don't succeed alone—they have coaches. Top musicians have instructors. Successful writers have editors.

They don't outsource the actual performance; they get expert guidance that helps them perform better themselves.

This coaching model represents a fundamentally different relationship from traditional agency work.

Instead of doing the work for you, **a coaching-focused agency teaches you how to do the work and provides feedback to help you improve**. They train your team, share best practices, and help you develop systems that work for your unique situation.

As you slowly bring your marketing functions in-house, you need a guide—and that's the role an agency can fill. Rather than the typical outsourced "done-for-you" model, they become teachers and advisors who help your team grow their capabilities.

The Rise of Fractional CxOs

But what if you're not ready to hire a full marketing team, yet still want more control than an agency relationship provides?

There's another option that offers the best of both worlds: **Fractional support.**

A Fractional CMO or Marketing Director is an experienced marketing leader who works with your company part-time, typically for a set number of hours each week or month.

Unlike an agency that takes over execution, a fractional leader provides strategic direction and helps you build your marketing function the right way. They can help you:

- Develop a marketing strategy aligned with your business goals.

- Create systems and processes that scale as you grow.

- Hire and train the right people as your budget allows.

- Select and manage specialised agencies or freelancers when needed.

This approach gives you senior-level expertise without the full-time executive salary. It bridges the gap between having no marketing leadership and hiring a full-time CMO—which, for many growing businesses, is the perfect middle ground.

Reader's Resource: *Need hands-on marketing implementation without the full agency commitment?*

Scan this QR code to explore my Fractional Marketing Director service.

The Right Support For The Right Scenario

Does this mean you should never work with a traditional agency?

Not necessarily.

There are still situations where the standard agency model makes sense:

- When you need specialised technical expertise for a specific project.
- When you're entering a new market and need guidance from those who know it well.

- When you need to quickly scale production beyond your internal capacity.

The key is to enter these relationships with clear boundaries and an exit strategy. Use agencies to fill specific gaps while you build your internal capabilities, not as a permanent solution for all your marketing needs.

As you consider your marketing support options, remember that the goal isn't just to produce marketing materials, but to become better at marketing.

Every bit you spend should move you closer to self-sufficiency, not deeper into dependency.

The right approach combines learning with doing. Whether that means working with a coach, bringing in fractional leadership, or selectively using traditional agencies for specific projects, choose the option that builds your capabilities rather than just delivering temporary results.

This shift in thinking, from outsourcing your marketing to developing your marketing muscle, is what will ultimately create a sustainable competitive advantage for your business.

_____   *Chapter Summary*   _____

- The standard agency model often creates dependency rather than self-sufficiency, causing businesses to miss opportunities to build genuine trust with customers through authentic communication.

- External marketing support should help you become better at marketing yourself, not simply do the work for you—much like how elite athletes work with coaches who guide rather than perform.

- Fractional CMOs and Marketing Directors offer a middle-ground solution, providing senior-level strategic direction part-time without the full executive salary, helping you build systems and capabilities as you grow.

- Traditional agencies still have their place for specialised technical expertise, new market entry, or quickly scaling production, but these relationships should have clear boundaries and exit strategies.

- Every penny spent on marketing support should move you closer to self-sufficiency rather than deeper dependency, creating a sustainable competitive advantage through developing your own marketing capabilities.

CHAPTER 57

Futureproofing Your Content Strategy: Navigating the Ever-Changing Marketing Landscape

Remember when Netflix shipped DVDs in red envelopes?

I'm only just old enough to remember this, but I'm confident that there will be a generation of readers who aren't!

In the early 2000s, that simple mail-order service disrupted the entertainment industry.

Fast forward to today, and Netflix has transformed into a streaming giant with over 223 million subscribers worldwide, powered by smart algorithms and award-winning original content.

This transformation didn't happen by accident. Netflix spotted changing winds and adjusted their sails accordingly. Their evolution offers a valuable lesson for all of us trying to build trusted brands in a shifting landscape.

The content world is changing faster than ever before. Content may remain king, but the kingdom's rules keep changing.

As we close out this book, I thought it would be helpful to address the trends that we are facing, and how you can remain flexible enough to handle any major market shifts.

But first, let's be honest about the challenges. As we've established, **there is a massive trust deficit between brands and consumers, which only continues to widen**. Not only that, but buyer patience also keeps shrinking. If you don't capture attention quickly, you've lost it.

Buyer patience is one thing. We know buyer behaviour is changing too. Zero-click searches (from Chapter 24) continue to rise, with people finding answers directly in search results without visiting websites.

That's causing traditional SEO-focused websites to see declining visitor numbers, and traditional marketing agencies are struggling to deliver the same results they once did.

And let's not forget that there's more content competing for attention than ever before. Consumers are learning everywhere, with only 18% of all searches now happening on Google.

These challenges might sound daunting, but they present opportunities for brands willing to adapt.

The AI Revolution

30 November 2022 will go down in the history books for many. That was the day ChatGPT first graced our screens and started what is quickly becoming a tidal wave of change for sales and marketing teams alike.

But the shocking fact is that these current AI tools, though impressive, are only the beginning.

Think of today's AI like those bulky car phones from the 1970s and 1980s. There was a 40-year gap between those early mobile phones and today's smartphones, but AI will likely make a similar leap in just a few years.

I alluded to using AI tools in Chapter 50, but I want to delve deeper here. If you're thinking only about what today's AI tools can do, you're already falling behind. Whatever limitations you see today will likely be overcome next month.

Many marketers make the mistake of treating AI as a side project or a tool for specific tasks. **The smarter approach is to integrate AI into your everyday workflow** based on these four key principles:

1. Use AI in everything you do, every day. Just start using it consistently.

2. Be the human in the loop. The machine gives you options, but you provide judgement.

3. Communicate with AI as you would with a human and specify your needs clearly.

4. Remember that today's AI is the worst you'll ever use—it will only get better.

"But how do we use it?" you ask. Well, let's start with an easy answer: content creation.

As I said in Chapter 50, there is a flood of content being published that is lazy GPT-generated copy, with no edits or humanity added to it.

Yes, you can use AI tools for that. But the real AI connoisseurs will go much further. Here are a few examples:

- Generating multiple article outlines to find the best angle.

- Helping you rephrase your own ideas for clarity and impact.

- Fixing broken code on your website.

- Brainstorming fresh blog topics when you're feeling stuck.

- Analysing competitor content to find gaps you can fill.

And it doesn't stop there. Sales teams can benefit too, in the following ways:

- Analysing a prospect's background before a first call.

- Learning industry jargon quickly to speak a client's language.

- Practising sales conversations through role-play scenarios.

- Summarising lengthy communications for busy team members.

The key isn't just using AI to do what you already do, but to rethink how you work entirely.

Many professionals waste energy debating whether AI will replace their jobs. This is the wrong question to ask. Instead, **consider how AI can transform your work process**.

We've been working the same way for over a decade, trudging through mundane tasks that drain our creativity and energy. Using AI simply to research faster or create more content misses the bigger opportunity to fundamentally change how we work.

Those who view AI merely as a content production tool will fall behind. The real winners will be those who use AI to enhance their efficiency, creativity, and strategic thinking.

Changing Behaviours: Video and Voice Search

We also need to talk about the platforms that are reshaping content consumption, starting with YouTube. What started as a dating site has now become what television once was, but with even greater reach:

- 2 billion monthly users watching 1 billion hours of content daily.

- The dominant platform for podcasts, surpassing both Spotify and Apple.

- The world's largest music platform, with more music consumed on YouTube than on any dedicated streaming service.

- A key player in the buying journey, with 68% of shoppers using it for research before making purchases.

- A cornerstone of education, with 88.52% of instructors and 94.67% of students using YouTube in their educational activities.

YouTube is becoming the "University of Everything", a place where people learn everything from changing a tyre to understanding quantum physics.

And make no mistake: **the day is coming when your YouTube channel may be more valuable than your website**. The question is: are you ready for that shift?

It doesn't stop with YouTube. While it may be the mainstay for long-form content, YouTube Shorts, TikTok and Instagram are becoming powerhouses for short-form video. The same logic applies: education and research.

Voice search is also rapidly rising as a primary search interface. With smart speakers and digital assistants in millions of homes, our behaviour is changing from typing a query to asking the likes of Alexa. This behaviour is becoming the norm across all age groups.

This shift demands a different approach to content creation. People speak differently than they type. Voice searches tend to be longer, more conversational, and phrased as questions. "Best pizza London" becomes "Where can I find the best pizza in London?"

Smart content creators are now optimising for these conversational queries by:

- Structuring content around natural questions and answers.

- Creating concise, direct responses that digital assistants can easily pull.

- Focusing on local search terms, as many voice searches have local intent.

- Building structured data to help AI understand and present their content.

Reviews · Authority · Content · Reputation · **TRUST SIGNALS** · Social proof · Certifications · Security · Transparency

The Battle for Trust Signals

All these trends have a common denominator: signals.

The future of marketing isn't just about creating content. It's about generating trust signals.

Think of a signal as any digital touchpoint that communicates your brand's value and reliability.

Because AI systems are now scanning the internet, collecting and analysing these signals. Your content isn't just being judged by human readers and search engines—it's being assessed by AI too.

These signals come in many forms: customer reviews, photos of people using your products, survey responses, podcast mentions, infographics, guest posts, and dozens more. Each signal tells a story about your brand's trustworthiness.

So, as I said earlier in the chapter, yes, content remains king. But the content landscape will only get more complex. Each piece of content is another trust signal to be picked up.

Success belongs to those who can adapt, embrace the changes, and win the battle of trust signals. As you navigate these trends, remember that others will come and go, but quality content focused on customers will never go out of style.

Keep your eyes on the horizon and your feet on the ground. Welcome change with enthusiasm and empathy for the humans behind every screen and click. Content is simply a way to connect.

Master that, and no trend can derail your success.

Chapter Summary

- The content landscape is shifting dramatically with changing buyer behaviour, zero-click searches, and content being consumed across numerous platforms beyond Google—presenting both challenges and opportunities for adaptable brands.

- AI is transforming marketing at an unprecedented pace, and the wisest approach is to integrate it into your daily workflow as a collaborative tool that enhances your efficiency and creativity, rather than treating it as a mere content production shortcut.

- YouTube has evolved from a simple video platform into the "University of Everything", where consumers research purchases and learn new skills—potentially making your YouTube channel more valuable than your website in the near future.

- Voice search is fundamentally changing how people find information, requiring content creators to structure their material around natural questions and provide concise, conversational answers that digital assistants can easily extract.

- The future of marketing revolves around generating trust signals across multiple touchpoints, as both human readers and AI systems evaluate these signals to determine your brand's credibility and value.

CHAPTER 58

Show Your Worth: Demonstrating Content ROI (Return-On-Investment)

In 2019, Kraft Heinz stood at a crossroads.

Their traditional advertising was delivering less impact, so they needed a fresh approach to connect with customers and drive growth.

Their answer?

A complete content marketing strategy powered by a detailed ROI measurement system.

By tracking everything from leads generated to brand awareness to customer loyalty, Kraft demonstrated that their content efforts delivered four times higher returns than traditional advertising.

According to research from Aberdeen Group, companies that consistently measure content marketing ROI are 12 times more likely to see year-over-year increases in returns[27].

The message is clear: **what gets measured gets improved**.

But proving content's worth isn't just about convincing sceptical bosses or clients. It's about building a data-driven system that helps you make smarter decisions, optimise your resources, and steadily improve your content's impact.

Building Your ROI Framework

The first step to calculating content ROI is defining what success looks like for your business. This requires balancing direct revenue metrics with indirect value indicators:

Direct revenue metrics tell you exactly how much money your content is generating:

- **Lead generation**: How many qualified leads did your content produce?

- **Conversion rates**: What percentage of those leads became customers?

- **Sales influenced**: How much revenue was directly connected to your content?

- **Customer acquisition cost**: How much did you spend to acquire each new customer through content?

Indirect value metrics capture benefits that aren't immediately tied to revenue but still matter:

- **Brand awareness**: How many people saw and recognised your content?

- **Search rankings**: How well does your content rank for key search terms?

- **Social engagement**: How many likes, shares and comments did your content receive?

- **Customer loyalty**: How did content affect retention rates and customer lifetime value?

Once you've defined your metrics, the next challenge is connecting content to outcomes. This is where attribution modelling comes in.

The simplest models give all the credit to either the first touch—like the blog post that initially attracted a lead—or the last touch—like the case study that sealed the deal.

But these approaches ignore all the other content touchpoints that moved buyers through their journey.

Think of it like this: if you ask a friend how they heard about a new restaurant, they might mention the recommendation that finally convinced them to go.

But that doesn't account for the Instagram posts they saw, the reviews they read, or the menu they checked online. All those touchpoints played a role.

More sophisticated marketers use multi-touch attribution, which gives partial credit to each piece of content based on its role in the conversion path. Some companies even develop custom attribution models specifically designed for their business.

HubSpot's Powerful Attribution Tools

If you're using HubSpot (which we discussed in Chapter 54), you have several powerful options for tracking content ROI.

The most straightforward approach is setting up deal pipelines with actual revenue associated with individual contacts. When someone converts on your site, HubSpot automatically ties their information to the content pieces they interacted with.

This creates a direct line from specific blog posts, videos or downloadable resources to actual revenue.

For example, if someone reads your blog post about industry trends, downloads your ultimate guide, and then becomes a customer worth £50,000, you can trace that revenue back to those specific content pieces.

This works with ads too. HubSpot can show you which ads led to which deals, giving you clear ROI data for your paid campaigns.

For those with Enterprise HubSpot subscriptions, you gain access to even more sophisticated attribution models:

- First-touch attribution gives all the credit to the very first content piece a customer interacted with.

- Last-touch attribution credits the final piece of content before purchase.

- Linear attribution spreads credit equally across all touchpoints.

- Time-decay attribution gives more credit to more recent interactions.

- U-shaped attribution gives 40% credit each to the first and last interaction, with the remaining 20% spread across middle touchpoints.

Advanced Measurement Techniques

As your content strategy grows, so should your measurement capabilities. Leading businesses use techniques like:

- **Content scoring**: Assigning values to each piece of content based on performance, then focusing production on what works best.

- **Lifetime value calculation**: Measuring not just the initial sale, but the total projected revenue from a customer over their lifetime. This accounts for content's role in driving loyalty and repeat business.

- **Content efficiency ratio**: Calculating the revenue generated per amount spent on content, revealing opportunities to cut waste and scale winners.

- **Return on content investment (ROCI)**: A comprehensive formula that includes cost savings and productivity gains from content, along with direct revenue impact.

- **Predictive analytics**: Using machine learning to analyse past content performance and predict future results, enabling smarter planning.

While these advanced techniques require good data and technology, they provide unprecedented insight into content's true business value.

ROI Tracking Isn't Just About Money

When I tell businesses that they need to be tracking ROI, they often balk and think it's about micromanagement. Marketers even panic that their job is at risk if they can't prove their worth.

But ROI measurement is much more than that. **It provides you with the data for continuous improvement**. As competition for attention intensifies and pressure to deliver results increases, content marketers can no longer afford to fly blind.

By regularly analysing the performance of your content, you can make informed decisions about things like resource allocation, content prioritisation and, in turn, investment decisions.

Adobe offers a great example of ROI-driven optimisation. By implementing a sophisticated content attribution model, they identified blog posts, whitepapers and webinars that were outperforming benchmarks by 3x.

They used these insights to revamp their content calendar and reallocate resources, ultimately driving 50% higher conversion rates.

Your Path to ROI Mastery

ROI measurement is no longer optional. It's an essential practice for any content team serious about success.

So, if you're serious about mastering content ROI and building a measurement framework, here are the five steps you need:

1. Start with clear success metrics tied to business goals.

2. Implement solid tracking systems for both costs and results.

3. Develop an attribution model that reflects your unique customer journey.

4. Build dashboards that translate data into actionable insights.

5. Establish regular performance reviews and optimisation cycles.

Kraft Heinz's ROI revolution shows the transformative power of a well-built measurement framework. **By proving content's superior returns, they not only secured bigger budgets but changed the direction of their entire marketing strategy.**

As we've seen throughout this book, building a trusted brand through content requires understanding your audience, planning strategically, creating consistently, and focusing relentlessly on quality.

But without a clear view of the value content creates, even the best strategy will struggle to maintain support and investment.

ROI measurement is the linchpin that holds all the other elements together. It gives you the data to make smarter decisions, the insights to optimise your efforts, and the confidence to push your content programme to new heights.

I've seen this firsthand with dozens of businesses, from one-person operations to global enterprises. The companies that measure content performance systematically always outperform those that don't.

So, as you move forward with your content strategy, **make measurement a priority**. And use what you learn to make each piece of content better than the last.

The future of marketing belongs to those who believe in the power of content and can prove its worth. With the frameworks and approaches we've explored in this book, you're well prepared to lead the way.

May your metrics be clear, your attribution accurate, and your ROI ever increasing.

Chapter Summary

- Companies that consistently measure content marketing ROI are 12 times more likely to see year-on-year increases in returns, making measurement not just about proving worth but building a data-driven system for smarter decision-making.

- A comprehensive ROI framework balances direct revenue metrics (lead generation, conversion rates, sales influenced) with indirect value metrics (brand awareness, search rankings, social engagement, customer loyalty).

- Attribution modelling is crucial for connecting content to outcomes, with multi-touch attribution providing the most accurate picture by giving partial credit to each piece of content based on its role in the conversion path.

- HubSpot offers powerful ROI tracking capabilities, from basic deal pipelines tied to content interactions to sophisticated attribution models like first-touch, last-touch, linear, time-decay and U-shaped attribution.

- ROI measurement serves as the linchpin holding all content strategy elements together, providing the data for continuous improvement, smarter resource allocation, and confidence to secure ongoing investment.

CLOSING THOUGHTS
The Sea of Sameness

Let me share something uncomfortable: the marketing industry is broken.

But here's an even more uncomfortable truth: **we, the marketers, are the ones who broke it.**

We broke it through our obsession with copying others—through looking at competitors and thinking, "That looks good, let's do what they're doing!" Through chasing trends without understanding context, blindly replicating tactics without grasping strategy.

The result?

Genuine differentiation drowning in a sea of sameness.

Think about it: how many accountants have you seen doing advent calendars of finance tips? How many businesses jump on Black Friday discounts simply because "everyone else is doing it"? How many LinkedIn posts have you read that start with "Here's what [insert random event] taught me about [insert equally random and unrelated topic]..."?

The Cost of Conformity

Throughout this book, we've explored a different path. Not a path of imitation, but one of transformation. We've looked at how to:

- Transform your approach to buyer personas from demographic data to genuine understanding.

- Change your content from self-promotion to customer education.

- Shift your focus from features and benefits to honest transparency.

- Move from broadcasting to real engagement.

- Convert your sales process from pressure to partnership.

At every step, we've emphasised one crucial principle: the courage to be different.

The sea of sameness isn't just boring—it's dangerous.

lighthouse standing out

businesses drowning in someness

When every business sounds the same, looks the same and acts the same, we train our potential customers to make decisions based solely on price.

We commoditise ourselves.

We erase the very differentiation that could make us remarkable.

Think about the businesses we've studied throughout this book:

- River Pools and Spas dared to talk about cost, price and problems when others only talked about benefits.

- Patagonia had the courage to tell people not to buy their products.

- Drift recognised the natural storyteller sat right there in their business, a wealth of knowledge ready to be tapped into.

- Nike boosted their sales by understanding their core audience and their values, rather than targeting anyone and everyone.

None of these companies succeeded by copying their competitors. **They succeeded by daring to be different.**

As you've worked through this book, you've likely noticed a common thread woven through every chapter: **change.**

Not the superficial change like updating your logo or refreshing your website, or the tactical change like trying the latest social media platform.

But fundamental, strategic change in how you think about your customers, create and structure your content, build trust and ultimately, measure success.

This kind of change isn't easy.

It requires courage.

It demands commitment.

It means **standing out** when every instinct tells you to fit in.

The Path Forward

So here you are, at the end of this book, facing a choice—facing your own moment of truth:

Will you return to the safe harbour of sameness, doing what everyone else does because it's comfortable and expected?

Or will you chart a different course?

Will you be the business that writes the content your competitors are afraid to publish?

Will you have the conversations others avoid?

Will your business build the trust others only talk about?

But above all, will you make the changes others only contemplate?

The Trust BLUEPRINT™ framework I've shared isn't just another marketing methodology. No, it's an invitation to think differently about how you connect with your audience.

It's about being brave enough to be transparent when others hide, being helpful when others sell, and being trustworthy when others optimise for short-term gains. It's about being the changemaker your industry needs— the one who answers the questions others won't and shows the transparency that others fear.

The sea of sameness is vast, but it's not inescapable.

Every day, businesses break free by having the courage to be different, to be genuine, to be trustworthy.

There will be times where you want to resist, and if that feeling creeps in, remember this: we live in a world where everyone is trying to fit in, and the real opportunity lies in standing out.

The question becomes: will you be one of them? Are you ready to make that change?

The choice, as always, is yours.

Seeking Your Help and How to Reach Out

If you enjoyed this book, I would be incredibly grateful for a review on Amazon. I appreciate this may be a lot to ask, but it makes a massive difference in the success of this book and helps many other businesses in a similar situation to yourself start their own journey towards building a trusted brand.

And if you have any questions for me personally, just email me at tom@tomwardman.com.

Notes

Definition

1. Encyclopedia.com. (n.d.). Blueprint. *Encyclopedia.com* (blog). https://www.encyclopedia.com/science-and-technology/technology/technology-terms-and-concepts/blueprint

Chapter 10

2. HubSpot. (n.d.). How to create detailed buyer personas for your business. *HubSpot Blog*. https://blog.hubspot.com/marketing/build-buyer-personas

3. MarketingSherpa. (n.d.). Targeted persona content marketing strategy [Case study]. *MarketingSherpa Blog*. https://www.marketingsherpa.com/article/case-study/targeted-persona-content-marketing-strategy

4. UpReports. (n.d.). Buyer persona marketing: Why your customer is the new business model. *UpReports Blog*. https://www.upreports.com/blog/buyer-persona-marketing-customer-business-model

5. protocol80. (n.d.). 35 buyer persona statistics you need to know. *protocol80 Blog*. https://www.protocol80.com/blog/buyer-persona-statistics

Chapter 11

6. Schaefer, M. (2014, February 12). 31 business-building benefits of buyer personas. *{grow} Blog*.

https://businessesgrow.com/2014/02/12/31-business-building-benefits-buyer-personas/

Chapter 22

7. MarketingSherpa. (n.d.). Email marketing: Free paywall access [Case study]. *MarketingSherpa Blog.* https://marketingsherpa.com/article/case-study/email-marketing-free-paywall-access
8. Cropink. (n.d.). Lead generation statistics. *Cropink* Blog. https://cropink.com/lead-generation-statistics

Chapter 23

9. Sprout Social. (n.d.). The data behind social media connection. *Sprout Social Blog.* https://sproutsocial.com/insights/data/social-media-connection

10. Murray, J. (2018, July 10). Where are they now? Wendy's nuggets tweet and Carter Wilkerson. *Delish* (blog). https://www.delish.com/food-news/a22529419/where-are-they-now-wendys-nuggets-tweet-carter-wilkerson/

Chapter 24

11. Search Engine Land. (2024, March 19). Google Search zero-click study 2024. *Search Engine Land Blog.* https://searchengineland.com/google-search-zero-click-study-2024-443869

Chapter 26

12. Prefinery. (n.d.). Dropbox referral program: 3900% growth study. *Prefinery Blog.* https://www.prefinery.com/blog/dropbox-referral-program-3900percent-growth-study

13. LXA Hub. (2023, May 12). Sales and marketing alignment stats and trends 2023. *LXA Hub Blog.* https://www.lxahub.com/stories/sales-and-marketing-alignment-stats-and-trends-2023

Chapter 27

14. Brigham Young University. (n.d.). Will it blend? *BYU Magazine Blog.* https://magazine.byu.edu/article/will-it-blend/

Chapter 29

15. B2B Marketing. (2021, March 22). Straight line to concentric circles: The complex world of B2B buying in 2021. *B2B Marketing Blog.* https://www.b2bmarketing.net/straight-line-to-concentric-circles-the-complex-world-of-b2b-buying-in-2021/

Chapter 30

16. Mentor Group. (2023, July 14). The customer retention blueprint: Strategies for long-term success. *Mentor Group Blog.* https://www.mentorgroup.com/insights/the-customer-retention-blueprint-strategies-for-long-term-success

Chapter 31

17. Madison Logic. (2023, April 25). 15 must-know statistics about the importance of lead nurturing. *Madison Logic Blog.*

https://www.madisonlogic.com/blog/15-must-know-statistics-about-the-importance-of-lead-nurturing

Chapter 33

18. Twicsy. (2023, September 8). Content marketing statistics. *Twicsy Blog*. https://twicsy.com/blog/content-marketing-statistics

Chapter 34

19. Orbit Media. (2023, June 12). How to update old blog posts for SEO. *Orbit Media Blog*. https://www.orbitmedia.com/blog/update-old-blog-posts

20. Content Marketing Institute. (2023, October 4). B2B content marketing: Benchmarks, budgets, and trends. *Content Marketing Institute Blog*. https://contentmarketinginstitute.com/b2b-research/b2b-content-marketing-trends-research

Chapter 39

21. Edelman. (2019, January 22). Only one-third of consumers trust most of the brands they buy. *Edelman Blog*. https://www.edelman.com/news-awards/only-one-third-of-consumers-trust-most-of-the-brands-they-buy

Chapter 40

22. Siegel+Gale. (2017, February 6). Siegel+Gale unveils seventh annual Global Brand Simplicity Index. *Siegel+Gale Blog*. https://www.siegelgale.com/siegelgale-unveils-seventh-annual-global-brand-simplicity-index-brands-that-embrace-simplicity-enjoy-

increased-revenue-valuation-brand-advocacy-and-employee-engagement

Chapter 43

23.   Adobe. (n.d.). Adobe business blog. *Adobe Blog.*
      https://business.adobe.com/blog/

Chapter 47

24.   Edelman. (2023). Edelman Trust Barometer. *Edelman Blog.*
      https://www.edelman.com/trust/trust-barometer

Chapter 55

25.   Wyzowl. (2023). State of video marketing report 2023. *Wyzowl Blog.*
      https://www.wyzowl.com/sovm-results-2023/

Chapter 58

26.   Konstruct Digital. (2023, July 5). Content marketing statistics.
      Konstruct Digital Blog. https://www.konstructdigital.com/content-marketing/content-marketing-statistics

Acknowledgements

In 2017, *Build A Trusted Brand* was just a seed of an idea, known then as *The Marketing BLUEPRINT*. Certain colleagues were quick to dismiss it. "Focus on your job," they said!

Looking back, I owe those naysayers a peculiar thank you. Their doubt became the fuel that kept my pen moving when motivation waned. Their scepticism built my resolve, allowing me to publish the initial eBook version as *The Marketing BLUEPRINT* in 2020.

But that was just the beginning.

What started as *The Marketing BLUEPRINT* framework evolved into something far greater, despite the challenges life threw my way, including redundancies, a global pandemic, bereavements, and personal health battles.

This transformation wouldn't have been possible without those closest to me. While some tried to dim my light, others helped it shine brighter. They believed in this vision when I faced one setback after another, encouraging me to expand what began as a framework into the complete book you're holding today.

The journey hasn't been mine alone, though. My clients, partner communities, and supporters deserve profound thanks for holding me accountable and sparking fresh ideas along the way. Your trust in our work together has been the bedrock of this project.

Several remarkable individuals contributed their insights to these pages. Marcus Sheridan, Lyndsey Cambridge, and John Espirian—your stories and expertise have added immeasurable depth to this book. And to Bob Ruffolo, my sincere gratitude for writing the Foreword.

To my manuscript readers: Dia Vavruska, Josh Anderson, Arthur Swanson, Courtney O'Daniel, Lucas Doornhein, Charleh Knighton, Sharon Glenn, Jonathan Broadley, Marc Duke, Marta Checa, Meg Porter, Joe Daniels, Alex Grundy, Amy Peterson, Kate Tyson, Paul Kitchener, Antonino Cantone, and Gemma Graham—your time and feedback shaped this work in countless ways. The direction and accountability you provided turned rough ideas into polished thoughts.

Special recognition goes to Dia, Arthur, and Joe, whose exceptionally detailed feedback and revision suggestions elevated every chapter they touched.

Behind the scenes, this book benefited from exceptional professional support. In particular, my thanks go to Chryzia Coz, whose incredible design work brought life to every internal graphic—your visual storytelling enhanced these pages immeasurably.

To my family—both those I was born to and those who welcomed me as their own—thank you for your endless encouragement. Your belief in me through every twist and turn has been a constant source of strength.

And to my wife Lydia, my tulip—no words fully capture what your support has meant. Through each setback and triumph, you've been my unwavering guide, my truest friend, and my greatest supporter.

When I couldn't see the path ahead, your wisdom guided me forward, and your presence fills my world with indescribable happiness and love.

You are my rock, and this book simply wouldn't exist without you.

About the Author

Tom Wardman is a Fractional Marketing Director, CMO, and HubSpot Consultant who helps businesses build trusted brands that drive sustainable revenue growth through simple, proven systems.

Based in Hull, England, he was hand-selected to become an Endless Customers Certified Coach—one of fewer than 35 coaches worldwide to receive this accolade.

Since founding his fractional consultancy in 2023, Tom has provided a mix of done-for-you services, consultancy, and coaching to in-house sales and marketing teams globally, from investor-funded start-ups to global enterprise brands.

His approach combines over a decade of real-world marketing experience, drawing on valuable lessons learned both as an in-house marketer and while working with clients at agencies.

Through his strategic marketing approaches, Tom has helped businesses generate millions in revenue and transform their marketing from guesswork into reliable systems for growth.

When he's not transforming marketing strategies, Tom can often be found performing as a pianist for various tribute and wedding bands, applying the same passion and precision to music that he brings to his client work.

For Additional Help and Information

Tom offers several ways to help you implement the strategies from this book and build a trusted brand that drives sustainable growth:

- **Book Tom to Speak**: Tom delivers engaging keynotes and workshops on building trusted brands, navigating today's digital landscape, and creating marketing systems that drive measurable results. No theoretical fluff—just proven approaches with clear implementation steps. To book Tom for your event, email tom@tomwardman.com.

- **Fractional Marketing Support**: Whether you need complete marketing management as a Fractional Marketing Director or strategic guidance as a Fractional CMO, Tom provides the expertise to build trust with customers and drive growth. Perfect for businesses that want professional marketing support without hiring a full department.

- **Coaching and Training for In-House Teams**: Take back control of your marketing future. Start with a one-day Company Alignment Workshop to unite your team behind a clear marketing vision or commit to the comprehensive In-House Marketing Mastery program that gives your team everything they need to build trust and drive sustainable growth—without relying on agencies.

Learn more about these services at tomwardman.com or email tom@tomwardman.com to schedule a chat about your marketing goals.

Index

tom
wardman

Are you ready to build your trusted brand?

If you want to transform your marketing from scattered tactics into a systematic approach that builds unshakeable trust and drives sustainable growth, **Tom Wardman** can help.

Tom works with businesses to **create reliable marketing systems** that create trust and turn it into steady, predictable revenue growth. Together, you'll transform your marketing from guesswork into a clear path to endless customers.

His services are split into three paths to success:

- **Done-for-you marketing**: Expert marketing support that brings you steady leads while you focus on running your business
- **Done-with-you strategy**: Strategic guidance that helps your team create and execute marketing plans that drive growth
- **Done-by-you coaching**: Learn the systems and skills your team needs to master marketing and bring in customers on your own

Using the proven systems from this book and clear implementation steps, you'll create **marketing that consistently brings in quality leads**, turns them into loyal customers, and transforms your brand into your customers' trusted choice.

n the QR code to get in touch with Tom.